GENIUSHOUR

GENIUS HOUR

PASSION PROJECTS THAT IGNITE INNOVATION AND STUDENT INQUIRY

Andi McNair

PRUFROCK PRESS INC.
WACO, TEXAS

Library of Congress catalog information
currently on file with the publisher.

Copyright ©2017, Prufrock Press Inc.

Edited by Katy McDowall

Layout design by Raquel Trevino

ISBN-13: 978-1-61821-634-2

Printed in the United States of America.   •

At the time of this book's publication, all facts and figures cited are the most current available.
All telephone numbers, addresses, and websites URLs are accurate and active. All publica-
tions, organizations, websites, and other resources exist as described in the book, and all have
been verified. The authors and Prufrock Press Inc. make no warranty or guarantee concern-
ing the information and materials given out by organizations or content found at websites,
and we are not responsible for any changes that occur after this book's publication. If you find
an error, please contact Prufrock Press Inc.

Prufrock Press Inc.
P.O. Box 8813
Waco, TX 76714-8813
Phone: (800) 998-2208
Fax: (800) 240-0333
http://www.prufrock.com

Dedication

For my husband, John—thank you for supporting me as I chase my dreams and pursue my passions. You are my everything!

For my children, Cory, Eli, and Katy—you are the reason that I do what I do. I hope that you find your passions and chase your dreams, knowing that I'll be behind you every step of the way.

Table of Contents

Acknowledgments

It is with deepest gratitude that I thank each of the people below. The following individuals gave their time, advice, and love as I worked on my own Genius Hour project—writing a book to inspire educators to do what is best for their students.

My husband and sweet children—your patience and willingness to let me pursue my passion has been my strength, and I love you all so very much.

My parents—thank you for raising me to believe that I could do anything and encouraging me to do what I wanted even when it seemed impossible.

My sister, Mandi—thank you for sharing my passion with others and listening when I needed a friend. Your support means more than you will ever know.

My Bosqueville family—Kelly, Brenda, and the parents of my sweet students—thank you for trusting me and letting me do things that were outside of the box. Your willingness to let me incorporate Genius Hour changed everything. Brenda, thanks for being such a great life coach!

My Region 12 family—your support and help as we charter new waters has been such a blessing. Thank you for being a lighthouse for innovation in education and supporting educators to teach today's students.

Kari Espin—your friendship and passion for innovation in education is inspiring. I am so grateful for our conversations and great ideas!

My Genius Hour family—I am so thankful to be a small part of a community that believes in giving students opportunities to chase their dreams, create the future, and change the world. You inspire me!

Katy McDowall—thank you for your patience and guidance throughout this entire process. I could not have done it without you!

Section I
Introduction

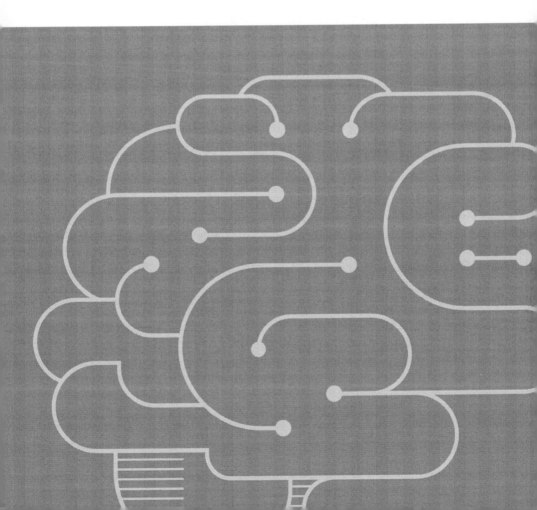

Chapter 1

Why Passion Projects?

BIG IDEA

If what we are teaching in the classroom is not meaningful, it is a waste of our time and theirs.

"I'm so excited about this!"

"I wish I could've done something like this when I was in elementary."

"I want to innovate and be challenged . . . my mind is constantly spinning with ideas."

These are just a few of the comments I heard when I shared our Genius Hour projects with students who visited my classroom last year. They were gifted high school students who came to the elementary school once a week to work with my gifted students, and they were so impressed with what and how my students were learning. They could not believe that I was allowing my students to work freely on whatever they wanted. They were astonished and began to ask questions, wanting to know more about how and why this worked in my classroom.

Four years ago, I found my passion teaching gifted education in a small, rural district in Texas. About 3 years ago, I began to realize that my students needed something more. They needed a way to tap into their passions and do something that would make a difference to their learning and beyond. Coincidentally, I came across Don Wettrick, author of *Pure Genius: Building a Culture of Innovation and Taking 20% Time to the Next Level*. He was sharing about his innovations class on "The Two Guys Show," an educational webcast (Minock, 2013). As I listened to him share about the experiences that he was offering his high school students, I couldn't help but realize that it was exactly what my students and I were missing. I remember a specific moment in the webcast when Don said, "There's never been a better time to be student."

As I listened and learned, I was so excited because I began to understand that while that was so very true, there has also never been a better time to be teacher. I needed to make learning more personal, more real, and more engaging for my students. I had the technology and the tools to do so. So, I did. We jumped in with both feet. Passion projects became a priority in our classroom, and Genius Hour gave my students the opportunity to pursue things that matter to them. In doing so, they became creative thinkers, collaborative classmates, ambitious dreamers, and confident learners.

What Is Genius Hour?

So, what is a passion project? What is Genius Hour? And why do I believe that this type of learning has the power to change education as we know it?

It's really quite simple. Students choose a topic, a passion, or an interest. My students designed projects to learn more about animation, website design, animals, homelessness, sewing, and the list goes on. Whatever a student chooses to learn about becomes his or her project. Students then spend their time researching information, learning by doing, collaborating with experts, and designing a product that can be shared with an authentic audience. Although Genius Hour is what we called this time in my classroom, many classrooms prefer *passion projects* or *20% time*. Regardless of what it is labeled, it is a time for students to explore their passions through the creation of a product to share with the world.

Genius Hour has given my students the opportunity to pursue things that matter to them.

Let's be honest. Our students are tired. They are tired of learning by completing worksheets that involve nothing more than putting pencil to paper and regurgitating what they have just heard. They are tired of sitting in classrooms quietly while the rest of the world collaborates and communicates in order to find success. They are ready to be seen as the learners that they are. It's time to realize that in our classrooms sit the world changers, inventors, and innovators of tomorrow. Our students are the future. If they are indeed our future, then why are we still trying to force them to learn in the same ways that we have in the past? It doesn't make sense.

Why Genius Hour?

Passion projects give students an opportunity to learn by doing. Application of the standards is the best way for students to gain understanding. By applying the standards, they begin to see real-world connections and understand that their learning can go beyond the walls of the classroom. None of us want to spend any of our time doing meaningless work. Instead, we want our work to be relevant. We want to make a difference, ignite change, and be engaged in meaningful learning. As teachers, we should want nothing less for our students. If what we are doing in our classrooms is not meaningful, it is a waste of our time and theirs.

Genius Hour provides students with opportunities to discover what it means to think for themselves, to really pursue something that is meaningful to them. It changes the role of the teacher and gives the learning back to the learners. It opens doors for students to have experiences that help them realize learning doesn't have to be done by choosing A, B, C, or D. Instead, students will design projects that are personally significant and engaging.

It's time to realize that in our classrooms sit the world changers, inventors, and innovators of tomorrow. Our students are the future.

Genius Hour doesn't mean that students are working and we, as teachers, sit back and hope that they are learning something. Our role has simply changed. Instead of designing a one-size-fits-all lesson for our students, we teach by questioning and finding creative ways to weave the standards into each one of our students' projects. We engage in conversations that help our students make connections and see the learning that might have been missed without our insight.

We tend to make a lot of assumptions in education. We assume that our students will not be motivated enough to learn independently. We assume that teachers will see things like Genius Hour as "one more thing." We assume that administrators will not allow us to implement something like this in our own classrooms. It's time to stop making assumptions and start doing what is best for our students.

Forbes magazine recently published an article on the "10 Skills Employers Most Want in 2015 Graduates." In the article, Susan Adams (2014) explained that working well on a team, solving problems, communicating with others, and making decisions are some of the most important skills when looking for employment. The other skills include:

- the ability to plan, organize, and prioritize work;

- the ability to obtain and process information;

- ① the ability to analyze quantitative data;

- ① technical knowledge;

- ① proficiency with computer programs;

- ① the ability to create and/or edit written reports; and

- ① the ability to sell and influence others (para. 3).

It's time to stop making assumptions and start doing what is best for our students.

As educators, are we preparing our students appropriately? Are we giving them opportunities in the classroom to solve problems in creative ways or are we expecting them to come in every day and "play school"? How many of our classrooms give opportunities for students to work as a team instead of the dreaded group work that results in one or two students carrying the load while knowing they will all receive the same grade? How often do we engage our students in real conversation apart from calling on them to answer a question or giving them permission to use the restroom? Do we really value their decisions or do we make decisions for them and expect them to react accordingly? The real world is telling us what it needs from our students. In order for us to prepare our students for the roles that they will fulfill in the future, classrooms have to change. We must begin to see our classrooms as a launchpad for our students and realistically prepare them for a future that is constantly changing.

How to Use This Book

In this book, I hope to explain passion projects in a way that will make the process easy to implement in any classroom. In an effort to help my students stay on track, I came up with a simple strategy that guides students through each step of a passion project. Throughout the book, I will explain each of the 6 P's of Genius Hour—passion, plan, pitch, project, product, and presentation—to be used as a map for students to follow as they create, design, and carry out a project.

As we take a look at each of the steps, I will share the technology, tips, and tricks that I found to make this process meaningful for my students and manageable for myself. I will share the importance of outside experts, authentic audiences, and meaningful reflection with suggestions of how to best create these experiences for your students. Each chapter includes a "big idea" or a major takeaway from that section and reflection questions to spark ideas and conversation. Throughout, you will also find strategies for quick implementation of each of the 6 P's, example student handouts, and strategies for using Genius Hour with gifted students. Full-size versions of any handouts are available on the book's webpage at http://www.prufrock.com/Assets/ClientPages/Genius_Hour.aspx. Finally, the end of the book includes a list of additional resources about Genius Hour and a compiled list of the technology tools discussed throughout the book.

I'm so excited that you have decided to join me in pursuing passion in the classroom. My hope is that when you put this book down, you will realize the importance of giving the learning back to our students. Genius Hour is an opportunity that every student deserves. Whether it's a student in your classroom who struggles with traditional learning, a student who has great ideas and just needs an opportunity to make those ideas a reality, or a student who sits in your classroom waiting for his or her chance to do something great, giving students the freedom to learn by doing changes everything. Finally, I hope that Genius Hour ignites your own passion for teaching. Whether you are frustrated, bored, or even if you love your job and just long for more for your students, I hope that this book and the simple strategies that I share will meet you where you are and change your classroom to be more than you could have ever imagined.

Reflection Questions

1. Do you believe that it is an exciting time to be an educator? Why or why not?

2. How could Genius Hour change the atmosphere of your classroom?

3. Are you comfortable with your role as an educator changing? What makes you the most uncomfortable?

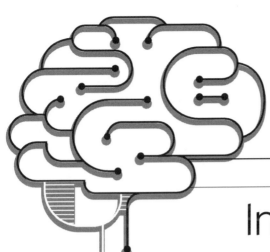

Chapter 2

Introducing the 6 P's

BIG IDEA

Genius Hour is a mess. It's our job to make that mess meaningful.

So, I'm not going to lie. Passion projects can be a mess. Genius Hour in my classroom often looked like complete chaos. A typical day in my classroom involved students sewing, painting, building models, and creating websites. To say the least, we had a lot going on.

As I began to really watch my students as they went through the Genius Hour process, I began to realize that they were struggling to find their way. They would get lost in the project portion, and this resulted in frustration and even anxiety for some of my students. I was constantly being asked, "What do I do now?" or hearing statements like "I don't know what to do next." Because they weren't sure where to go next, many students either gave up or used their time working on things that were not going to result in a final product. Projects were ending before they really began, and my students were not finishing what they had started.

Many students, especially gifted students, struggle with the open-endedness of Genius Hour. They often ask what they are expected to do or if they are doing it "right." The ambiguity and vagueness of the assignment can often bring anxiety and uncertainty. Because many of these students are afraid of failure and afraid of doing something wrong, Genius Hour can definitely be aggravating and even upsetting. Those students who want to please worry that their project will not live up to what is expected, and those who see things in black and white become frustrated when they are told there is not a "right" answer.

I knew that there had to be a way for my students to find their way through the process while still taking ownership of their projects.

I can remember being so excited about Genius Hour and expecting my students to be super excited as well. As we first began talking about exploring our passions and learning in our own ways, of course they were excited. However, as it began to sink in that they were going to be responsible for their own learning, the panic came. Students started to understand that they were going to have more ownership than ever before, and that was scary. What once was excitement soon became concern and almost fear of the unknown. They had never learned this way, and they weren't quite sure they were willing to give up that comfort zone of me telling them what to do and how to do it.

That discomfort helped me realize the importance of this type of learning. I began to see that my students needed me to stop doing things for them, and they needed the freedom to start being independent learners. It was time to let go and let them spread their wings. I knew there would be failure ahead and lots of mistakes, but I also knew that my students to deserved more than a canned curriculum that was not resulting in engaged learners who actively wanted to be in my classroom each day.

Introducing Genius Hour and working through the struggle was definitely a struggle within itself. However, because I believe in Genius Hour and I knew that I wanted this experience for my students, I refused to give up. I knew that there had to be a way for my students to find their way through the process while still taking ownership of their projects. Although I was okay with them finding their own way and making their own path, I also wanted them to find ways to be successful even if that success involved a few failures along the way.

Discovering the 6 P's

After struggling with Genius Hour for 2 years and knowing that I really needed to find a process, I literally woke up in the middle of the night and realized that every one of the steps that we were using began with the letter P. We started each project by finding our *passion* and then began to *plan*. In order to get peer feedback, my students would *pitch* their projects to the class before getting started. Then, they started working on the *project*. Finally, each project ended with a final *product* to share with the world and a *presentation* to share with the class what each student had learned. And there they were—the 6 P's—passion, plan, pitch, project, product, and presentation!

I couldn't go back to sleep because of all of the thoughts going through my head. I began to think about how much easier this would make the process for my students and how these 6 P's could serve as a map for a successful Genius Hour project.

Table 1 details the Genius Hour process using the 6 P's and the roles I took in implementing the process in my classroom.

Introducing the 6 P's to Your Students

There is a skill to building a fire. In order to build a fire that will actually burn, there are things you must do before lighting it to ensure that it will burn and provide warmth for everyone that sits around it. Typically, we gather the wood, build a small fire pit, stack the sticks, and then light the fire. It's not a difficult process, but if one of these steps is left out, it's possible that the fire will not be lit or will not burn as long or strong as we had hoped.

Table 1

The Teacher's Role in Implementing the 6 P's

Passion	Use observation and conversation to help students find their passion, and encourage self-awareness by allowing them to pursue it.
Plan	Encourage students to plan and prioritize as they make decisions about when and how specific tasks will be done as they design their project.
Pitch	Give students the tools and time to share their ideas with the class, and build classroom culture by allowing them to offer feedback and advice to their peers.
Project	Allow students to collaborate with outside experts, work through failure, and use what is needed to work on their project during the time that is provided.
Product	Share student products on social media, school websites, or newsletters to encourage self-promotion and help them understand the value of their work.
Presentation	Encourage students to work on communication skills as they share their project successes and failures with the class and others outside of the classroom.

The same is true for Genius Hour. Each one of the 6 P's is an important part of the process and plays a role that is vital to a project's success. When the 6 P's are introduced to students, it is important that they realize and really understand each step and the reasons why it is relevant to the Genius Hour process. Figure 1 is an example of a handout I use to introduce my students to the 6 P's.

Student Name:_____ Date:_____

Genius Hour 6 P's

1. **Passion:** What do you want to learn about? What do you think is interesting? What can you get excited about?

2. **Plan:** Who will be your outside expert? What materials will you need to complete the project? What will you need to do each day to reach your goals?

3. **Pitch:** How will you share your idea with the class? How will you get us on board?

4. **Project:** It's time to dive in! What do you need to do today to move forward with your project? What are you creating, making, or designing?

5. **Product:** What did you create? What can you show us to demonstrate your learning?

6. **Presentation:** How do you plan to share your learning? Can you share your idea or project with others? What tools will you use to make your presentation engaging for the audience?

Figure 1. Sample student handout introducing the 6 P's.

Integrating the 4 C's + 1 R

The 4 C's—collaboration, communication, creativity, and critical thinking (National Education Association, 2010)—have been a priority in my classroom since I became a connected educator. As teachers, it is so important that we understand the impact that these skills can have on our students. These are the skills that they will need as they prepare for the future. In my classroom, we liked to refer to these skills as the 4 C's + 1 R. Reflection is just as important and must play a role in learning.

The 6 P's give us an opportunity to purposefully engage our students in activities that encourage the use of these skills. Each step requires them to think beyond themselves and outside of their comfort zones. Each part of the process is intentionally designed to strengthen collaboration skills, offer opportunity for communication, engage students in critical thinking, inspire creativity, and encourage reflection.

4 C's + 1 R

- Collaboration
- Communication
- Creativity
- Critical Thinking
- Reflection

As you read, you will find that each chapter includes several ways for you to introduce each step to your students. I have included several technology tools that will help your students make connections and understand what each step involves. I hope that the personal stories that I share will encourage you and enable you to see the reality of Genius Hour. The reality is that although it's not always easy and sometimes even frustrating, it gives our students an opportunity to do something amazing. It gives them a voice, an outlet.

A gifted high school student once told me that he would have given anything to be able to pursue his passions. He explained that he had so much going on in his mind all of the time that it was diffi-cult for him to focus. If he had been able to engage in something like Genius Hour as an outlet for all of those thoughts and ideas, I would be willing to bet that he would have been able to clear his mind and find that focus that he knew he needed. I am a firm believer that student voice is so much more important than we, as adults, think or assume.

As you read this book, the reflection questions at the end of each chapter will help you think about your own classroom. Reflection is such an important part of the learning process and reflecting will help you understand what will and will not work for you and your students. As you think about each question, be honest and willing to think differently about your classroom. It might be a good idea to document your responses as you read and refer back to those responses throughout this journey.

My hope is that this book will make it easy for you to implement this process into your classroom. I want to make it as easy on you as possible so that you can find time to focus on the conversations and interaction with your students that is absolutely vital in order for Genius Hour to be a success.

So, sit back, grab a snack, and let's talk about each one of the steps in the 6 P's of Genius Hour. In the next chapters, I will care-fully explain what each step means, how it works, and what it should look like in the classroom. As you read, think about your students. Think about the potential each step has to change and transform your classroom into a place where students are given opportunities to be themselves, learn by doing, and possibly change the world.

Reflection Questions

1. Do you see value in addressing the 4 C's + 1 R (collaboration, communication, creativity, critical thinking, and reflection) in the classroom? Are those skills a priority in your classroom? How can you make them a priority?

2. Do you think any of the 4 C's are more valuable than the others? If so, which one(s) and why?

3. Are you okay with messy learning? Do you believe that messy learning can be meaningful?

Section II
The 6 P's

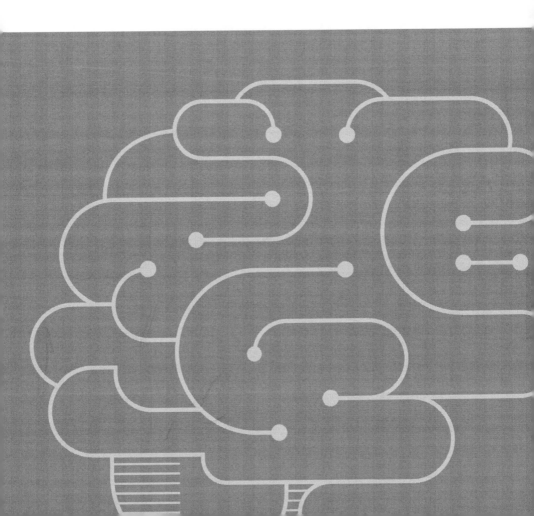

Chapter 3

Passion

Finding the Spark

BIG IDEA

Every student has a passion; it's up to us to help them find that passion and pursue it.

When was the last time you visited a Kindergarten classroom? If you teach any grade level above third grade, I would encourage you to do this. Just drop in and take a look around. Watch the students' faces, listen to their conversations, and count the number of times that someone asks a question. I would be willing to bet that you will be smiling before you the leave the room.

After visiting, reflect on what you observed and compare it to your own classroom. Even if you teach 12th-grade English, think about the differences. What did you notice? What did you see, hear, and feel? Of course, there are obvious differences such as behavior, vocabulary, and problem solving skills. But ask yourself, "Do my students still ask questions, learn by doing, and take risks?"

> What if there was a way to teach the standards by giving them opportunities to learn by making, creating, and even designing?

If we were honest, most of us would have to say no. Instead our students wait for us to tell them what to learn, how to learn it, and when it should mastered. They have lost that spark for learning. That spark that we observe in Kindergarten and first-grade classrooms has fizzled out—it's gone. Of course, there are your rare cases of students that simply love to learn and never lose that spark. But, generally speaking, you do not see too many fifth-grade students asking, "What if?" Or "Why not?" Instead you see them solving the problem the same way as it was done on the board and doing it 25 times to prove mastery on a worksheet. Are we really okay with that? Is this really what we want in our classrooms?

What if our students could learn by exploring their own passions, interests, and questions? What if there was a way to teach the standards by giving them opportunities to learn by making, creating, and even designing? I'm sure that regardless of your teaching philosophy, you can imagine the impact that this type of learning could have on our students. And although it sounds like a great idea, it also sounds really scary and risky. Our minds immediately go to our checklist of standards and test preparation.

The majority of us did not get into teaching to hand out worksheets and assign lunch detention. We focused on education because we love children, realize the potential to impact the future, and want to make a difference. But then it happened. We became complacent, comfortable, and satisfied with just doing enough. We realized that we couldn't beat the system, and that year's test scores determined our worth. Year after year, we continue to look for the "magic pill" to reignite our classrooms.

> *Passion* is defined as a strong feeling of enthusiasm or excitement for something or about doing something. It's a fire that burns within that can't be extinguished.

I'm not sure that there is anything more powerful than passion. Think about your own passions. Understand that I am not talking about hobbies or activities; I am talking about passion. *Passion* is defined as a strong feeling of enthusiasm or excitement for something or about doing something. It's a fire that burns within that can't be extinguished. I enjoy sewing, but it's not my passion. It's fun, and I will do it in my spare time, but it's not something that occupies my thoughts or keeps me up at night. However, encouraging educators to begin to see their classrooms differently is my passion. I think about it often, lying awake at night thinking of ways to make a difference, and spend my free time researching, reading, and taking in any information that I can regarding innovative teaching strategies. I am passionate about it. It's important enough to be a priority.

Discovering Your Students' Passions

What are your students' passions? Many of us have no idea. You may know that Johnny likes racecars, but do you know that he goes home and works on cars with his dad? Do you know that he sees the inside of car like a puzzle and loves putting them back together after they have been taken apart? Johnny thinks about cars in class. He draws them, peruses car parts online in the computer lab when no one is looking, and would give anything to have time during the school day to share this passion with anyone who would listen.

Finding our students' passions is not an easy task. Most of the time, they do not even know what they want to learn more about. It is a matter of finding that spark, which requires us to know our students well. Listening to what they talk about, knowing what they read, and watching what they search online can all help us as teachers find their spark. They know what they enjoy, but not what they are passionate about. Understanding passion has to be taught and then encouraged. Our questions and conversations with our students can be the match that lights the spark.

> # The only way that we can truly know our students is through conversation and observation.

In order to help our students find their passions we must first know our students. We cannot know our students by grading their worksheets. We cannot know them by simply saying "Good morning" at the door each day but then not speaking to them again unless we are calling on them or reprimanding their behavior. The only way that we can truly know our students is through communication and observation. Talk to them, ask them questions, and engage them in meaningful conversation. In my classroom, conversation trumped everything. Offering genuine feedback is so much more meaningful and beneficial than a grade written in red pen on a paper. A student-teacher conference means so much more than a report card full of A's and B's. Conversation always wins.

Observation is also important. Recess is a great place to begin to realize your students' passions. Perhaps Jessie spends her recess making dog toys out of recycled materials, while Michael spends his time teaching other students how to throw a football correctly. Many of us initially think these things don't happen during our recess. My students just run around and act like kids. But just look around. The next time you take your class outside, walk around and listen to their conversations. Swing next to Sally and ask about her activities outside of school. Watch her face and take note of her reactions. Did she smile when she talked about helping her mom cook dinner every night? Observation and conversation—if you want to know what your students' passions are—have to be the starting point.

How to Help Your Students Realize Their Passions

When I introduced passion in the classroom, I loved to ask my students to fill out a bracket just as they would for March Madness (see Figure 2). I got this idea from A. J. Juliani (2013), and it works so well. It really helps students think about what their passions are versus their interests. They may have 64 interests, but when the bracket is completed, what wins?

Figure 3 is an example of a bracket that was completed by one of my students.

Let's be honest. When you first hand out a bracket like this, your students are going to say things like, "I don't know what I like" and "Can you just tell me what to write?" And we can't blame them. This is what they know school to be. They are familiar with us telling them what to do and how to do it. The first time the tables are turned and we begin to give them the freedom to explore their own interests, they are going to be uncomfortable. It's like putting on a shoe that's too big, too much room. It doesn't fit right now but with time, they will grow into it.

Online Resources for Students to Find Their Passions

There are many tools that I introduced to my students to help them find their passions along the way.

Wonderopolis (http://wonderopolis.org) is a wonderful way for students to begin to realize what they want to learn about. I introduced this website to my students in first and second grade. I asked them to pay attention to what they tend to search. For example, do you always look for wonders about robots or LEGOs? Or do you

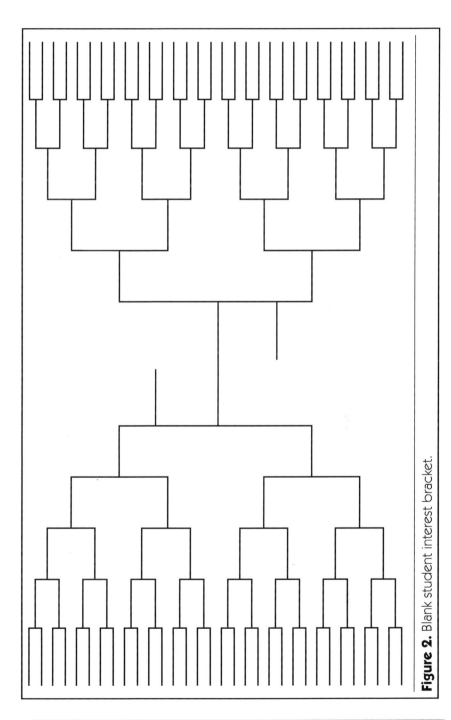

Figure 2. Blank student interest bracket.

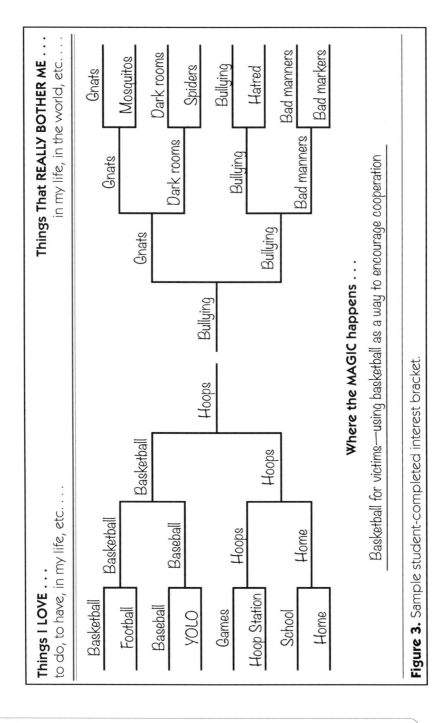

Figure 3. Sample student-completed interest bracket.

like to learn about marine animals? Wonderopolis is such a great tool as it offers choice. Students can choose from thousands of wonders, decide whether or not they need it read to them, and even click on difficult words for a definition.

I often suggest that teachers give students an index card every time they visit Wonderopolis. Ask them to write their name and the name of the wonder on the top of the notecard. Instead of doing the Wonder of the Day, allow them to search for wonders that are of interest to them. After they have read the wonder, they can click "Did You Get It?" and answer the questions about what they have just read. Collect these notecards over a period of time. After students have completed a few wonders, take a look at the cards. It's probable that you will see a pattern in the wonders that each student has chosen to explore. Katy may have read wonders about dogs, cats, birds, and veterinarians. It's clear that she is interested in learning more about animals and might even be passionate about the subject. Coltyn may search wonders about robots, cell phones, and 3-D printers. It is evident that he is interested in technology and might find his passion here.

DIY (https://diy.org) is another tool that makes it easy to for students to explore their options. This website offers many different "skills" to students. They simply decide on a skill, such as fashion designer, architect, paleontologist, or web designer. There are so many skills for them to choose from that they would be hard pressed to say they could not find anything. After finding a skill that sounds interesting, students can find challenges that will help them master that skill. As they complete the skills, students earn digital badges as they work toward becoming a master. DIY gives students an opportunity to realize that many of their passions can become careers and is a great place to start as students begin to explore.

> Passion requires our students to be creative. They must think differently about themselves, their motives, and their peers.

Finally, DOGO News (http://www.dogonews.com) is a place for students to read about real things going on in the world. It is a collection of current events for kids. In looking at this website, students begin to sense the difference that they can make. For example, they may read an article about the battery of the future being invented from paper (Feitlinger, 2016) and realize that they would love to invent things or create something new. They may be inspired to find other ways to make batteries or learn how batteries really work. As a side note, the subscription version of DOGO News articles includes article comprehension questions and a critical thinking question at the end of each article. This is such a great tool to use in the classroom.

All of these tools just get the wheels turning. They help students realize that there is a world outside of the classroom. Passion requires our students to be creative. They must think differently about themselves, their motives, and their peers. I absolutely love it when a student says that he or she doesn't have a passion and the entire class responds because they know that student well enough to know exactly what his or her passion is.

Passion is a big hurdle. As a teacher, it can be frustrating and time consuming to help every student find his or her passion. However, when your students find it and you see their eyes light up or they come to you and ask to stay in at recess to do more research on the topic, it's clear that something very different is happening. The tide has shifted and everything is about to change. Because once a student finds that passion, there's no turning back. By giving students an opportunity to find their passion, you have found a spark. And we all know that where there's a spark, there's fire. Now it's time to start building that fire and give students the tools to keep it going.

Reflection Questions

1. Do you value your students' interests and passions in the classroom?

2. Do you believe that every student deserves an opportunity to pursue his or her passion during school hours?

3. Think about some of the students in your classroom. Do you know what they are interested in, what they are passionate about?

PASSION

Quick Tips for Implementation

1. Listen to your students. Have conversations with them and listen to understand.

2. Observe your students during unstructured activities. Pay attention to what they do when they don't know you are watching and talking about when they don't know you are listening.

3. Use technology to expose students to new ideas and project suggestions.

The Technology to Make It Happen

DIY
https://diy.org

DOGO News: Fodder for Young Minds
http://www.dogonews.com

Wonderopolis
http://wonderopolis.org

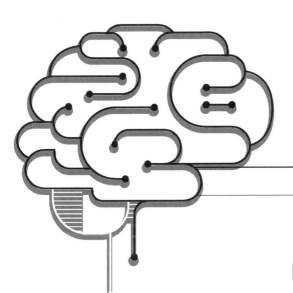

Chapter 4

Plan

Building the Fire

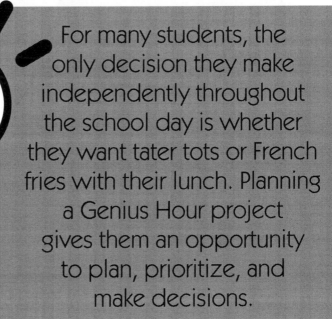

BIG IDEA

For many students, the only decision they make independently throughout the school day is whether they want tater tots or French fries with their lunch. Planning a Genius Hour project gives them an opportunity to plan, prioritize, and make decisions.

Planning the project is an important step that will affect the success of the project as well as the work that the students do as they complete the project. If you don't build the fire, you can't light the match. Without this step, a passion project cannot go anywhere. It's just a jumbled mess of ideas and information with no purpose. Many students will not understand this step in the beginning and will want to move right into working on their project. However, after working on their plan, they will begin to realize that it is just as important, if not more so, as any of the other steps.

When introducing this step to students, it might be a good idea to give the example of planning a vacation. If you go on a vacation and have no plans, things might not go well. For example, if you don't plan the route that you will take, you don't know where you are going. If you do not reserve a hotel, you will have extra work to do once you arrive. The same is true for planning a project. If we don't plan the path that we want to take, we might get lost and lose our way. If we do not know what we are trying to accomplish, we might end up doing extra work that doesn't need to be done.

> The planning stage allows students to take control of their idea and gives them the freedom to decide what needs to take place, when things need to be done, and how they will make it happen.

Students are not often given the opportunity to make decisions and prioritize during the school day. Instead, we make decisions for them, telling them what to do and how to do it. As teachers, it's just easier to be specific and make sure every student knows what is expected. The planning stage of a Genius Hour project allows students to take control of their idea and gives them the freedom to decide what needs to take place, when things need to be done, and how they will make it happen.

There are three main questions that a student needs to answer in the planning process:

1. What am I trying to accomplish?

2. Who is my audience?

3. Who can help me as I work toward my goal?

Answering these basic questions in the planning stage will give students a path to follow and a plan to refer back to when they lose focus or become distracted. Planning a Genius Hour project should also include a KWH (What I Know, What I Want to Know, and How I Am Going to Find Out) chart, list of potential failures, plans for materials, outside expert ideas, and a timeline. Figure 4 is an example of a Genius Hour planning handout I use with my students.

Types of Projects

In order to know what they are trying to accomplish, students must look at the big picture. Is their work a service project, a learning project, or a design project? A service project is a project that will serve others in some way. I once had a third-grade student who created a campaign to collect scarves for the homeless. Over the Christmas break, we delivered the scarves and spent time at our local homeless shelter.

Student Name:_____ Date:_____

Genius Hour Planning Form

KWH

K	W	H
What Do I Know?	**What Do I Want to Know?**	**How Will I Find Out?**

What Materials Will I Need?

Materials I Will Bring	Materials I Will Need

Outside Experts

Who might be the expert on this topic, and how will we contact them?

Expert	Contact Information

Project Timeline

How long do you think your project will take?

_____

Figure 4. Sample student handout for Genius Hour planning.

Project Timeline, *continued*
How much time will you spend on your project each week?

_____

Potential Roadblocks

Potential Roadblock	Potential Solution

Pitch Day Plan
How will you pitch your idea to the class? Will you need technology, props, etc.?

_____

_____

_____

_____

Figure 4. Continued.

A learning project is a project that involves the student learning information about a specific subject. Writing a digital book about dolphins would be an example of this type of project. Students learn all that they can about a specific topic and then create something to share that information with others.

Designing and making is a favorite of my students and likely a type of project that many students will choose. A design project will result in something that is designed and then made by the student. Using Scratch (https://scratch.mit.edu) to design and then create a video game that can be played is a great example of a design/making project.

Authentic Audiences and Outside Experts

Knowing the purpose of their project gives students the ability to decide on their target audience. Is the project meant to teach younger students about a particular subject? Are they creating an app to share with developers? Are they designing a prototype for a new invention? A project is completed to share with an authentic audience. If there is not an audience, there is no purpose. Knowing the audience gives purpose and defines meaning as students work toward finishing the project.

Finally, students need to plan contact with an outside expert. In my opinion, this is one of the most important pieces of a Genius Hour project. This contact is what connects the learning to the real world. As students begin to think about who their outside expert will be, it is important that they understand that this cannot be Mom, Dad, or Uncle Joe. The expert has to be someone who will be beneficial in completing the project. If a student is writing a digital book about dolphins, their outside expert would not be someone who has been to SeaWorld. Rather, it would be someone who works with dolphins at SeaWorld.

There are many tools that students can use as they search for an outside expert. As we began to search for our experts, my students and I created a "Help Wanted" wall. In order to create the wall, we used Padlet (https://padlet.com). Padlet is basically a digital bulletin board that can be shared using a link. I created the board, and my students posted their projects and what they were looking far as far as an outside expert. Each student posted to the board with his or her name, a description of his or her project, and what he or she needed from his or her expert. Once all of the descriptions were posted, I shared the link with our district, our local colleges, and on social media. Sharing with our local colleges had a huge impact. Students from many different departments responded and even visited our campus to meet with my students and share their ideas. As my students met with the college students who volunteered to help, I began to realize the power of passion.

Two girls in my class created a high-tech collar to warn a dog when it was in danger. They were able to meet with a mechanical engineering student from Baylor University. She shared so much information on circuits and batteries and helped them make their remote control work properly. As I listened to her share, I began to realize that she was still passionate about mechanical engineering. I was not going to be passionate about batteries and circuits. But she was, and her passion fueled my students' excitement and helped them realize that mechanical engineering might be something to consider in the future. Let's be real, this type of learning would have never happened if I were simply teaching circuits from a textbook.

Using Padlet was a great way for us to contact experts while saving time. We connected a Google form to each card for the experts to fill out if they were interested in helping with the project. To make this process easier for me, I used the notification rules on the form to send me an e-mail when someone filled it out. This way, I didn't always have to check the form and keep up with who had responded. After someone filled out the form, I contacted them to gather information and set up a meeting time for my student. Because I taught elementary school, I was responsible for the contact. High school students, however, might be able to contact their own experts and set up their own appointments.

Nepris (https://nepris.com) is another way to find experts and set up meetings that will be beneficial for student projects. Although it is a paid subscription service, it is well worth the cost because of the quality of experts and the ease in setting up contact. In order to find an expert, you simply visit the website and tell it what you are looking for. Nepris also gives you an opportunity to select standards that you would like for the expert to address as he or she meets with your student. This is the perfect opportunity for students to connect content standards with the real world and find meaning in their learning.

Planning Tips and Tools

Throughout the planning stage, my students used many tools to create mind maps and project outlines. Popplet (http://popplet.com) is perfect for elementary students as it is very easy to use and simplifies the mind-mapping process. It gives them a space to plan their project and a visual to use for organization and idea production. Mindmeister (https://www.mindmeister.com) is another tool that students can use to organize their ideas and can be used as an add-on in Google Docs as well. Both of these tools give students a space to document the planning process.

At this point, my students also set up Trello boards (https://trello.com). Trello is a board that is made up of lists. Within each list, students can add cards with facts, ideas, or information. Trello is essentially the digital version of the notecards that many of us used to complete research when we were in school. My students set up their lists before they begin working on their projects. They then used Trello throughout the process to document their learning and save resources.

The first list I asked my students to create on their Trello boards is a KWHLAQ chart. KWH is a simple way to remember what I know, what I want to know, and how I am going to find out. LAQ stands for what I learned, what action I took, and what questions I still have (Tolisano, 2011). I have used KWH charts in the past but learned about KWHLAQ from Paul Solarz (2013) when we began Genius Hour in our classroom. As my students planned, they documented their KWH on their Trello boards so that they could refer back to it throughout the course of the project. The LAQ sections of the chart are completed at the end of the project.

The other lists are specific to subject areas such as math, science, social studies, English language arts, and technology. In the next chapter, I will share how students use these lists to document the standards that are being applied as they work on their projects.

Planning is an important skill that students need to practice. When they come to school every day and are told how to do things, when to do things, and why to do things, they become dependent on that and are unable to make decisions and plan things independently. This step in the 6 P's intentionally gives students the opportunity to work on this real-life skill while preparing to create something that is meaningful to them.

Reflection Questions

1. What opportunities do your students have to make decisions and prioritize throughout their school day?

2. Do you trust your students enough to let them take control of their project and make plans based on their vision?

3. Why is it important for students to learn to prioritize? How might this skill be beneficial in a real-world situation?

Quick Tips for Implementation

1. Help students understand why planning is such an important part of the process.

2. Have students complete a Genius Hour Planning Form (see Figure 4).

3. Introduce a variety of technology tools to help students document their plans.

The Technology to Make It Happen

Mindmeister
https://www.mindmeister.com

Nepris
https://nepris.com

Padlet
https://padlet.com

Popplet
http://popplet.com

Trello
https://trello.com

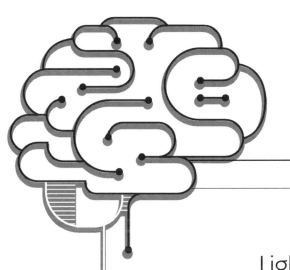

Chapter 5

Pitch

Lighting the Match

BIG IDEA

Building community in a classroom helps students connect and understand the purpose of collaboration.

I'll admit . . . I hate to camp. The only time that I really enjoy being outdoors is if I am at a baseball game or watching my kids play in the front yard. I definitely don't have the skills that it would require to survive the outdoors for any amount of time on my own. However, my husband loves being outside. He loves to camp and is always trying to convince me how much fun it is to enjoy and rely on the great outdoors.

I can remember campfires as a kid. I remember sitting around the fire in a circle and listening to one of our camp counselors share stories as we all listened. I remember sharing stories and conversations. As much as I don't enjoy camping now, I love those memories, and I think it's because it was such a feeling of community. We were all able to share, add to the conversation, and feel valued in that environment.

Pitch Day—when each student shares what his or her project will be—feels a little like a campfire to me. I look forward to hearing what each student has to share as well as everyone else's input, advice, and feedback for the projects as they are shared with the class. Pitch Day brings a sense of community into the classroom and helps everyone realize the importance of collaboration.

Collaboration is such an important skill and is very different than group work. Collaboration gives students an opportunity to really share and come together for a common purpose. Group work simply involves students working together to complete something for the teacher. Collaboration involves discussion, different ideas, suggestions, and even disagreement. Often times, group work is one-sided and completed by the student(s) who the group feels is most competent to earn the best grade. Many times, discussion in a group activity looks like this:

Student 1: What did you get for #1?

Student 2: I got A.

Student 1: Oh, I got C.

Student 2: Let's go with A because you're the GT student.

This is not collaboration. Just because students are talking and discussing does not mean that collaboration is taking place. True collaboration has to be learned, practiced, and encouraged. Students must feel safe and realize that their contributions and ideas can be appreciated by their peers.

I liked to explain collaboration by sharing the following scenario with my students:

> When my computer breaks at school, who do I call? I don't call the janitor, the secretary, or even the principal. I need to call the person on campus who will be able to help me, which would be someone in the IT department. Now, when an IT person arrives in my classroom, do I leave him or her to fix it without asking questions? No, instead I watch him or her fix it and ask questions as he or she does so, so that next time I can . . . ? Fix it myself.

In having this discussion, students realize the importance of knowing who in the classroom knows what. Making this connection will play a huge role in the Genius Hour process as they work on their projects.

Collaboration gives students an opportunity to really share and come together for a common purpose.

Pitch Day gives students an opportunity to really know each other well. If your students have truly found their passions, they will be so excited about sharing this information with their classmates. They will be bursting at the seams to share their ideas, their plans, and their intentions with their peers. Although sharing in front of their peers might bring anxiety, the experience in and of itself is so beneficial.

Developing Pitches

After students have decided on their passions and completed their planning, it's time to pitch their project to the class. Pitching a project will look different for different students. While some students are very comfortable talking and sharing with the class, others may be shy and hesitant to do something so outside of their comfort zones. This is why it is very important to offer student choice when students are preparing their pitches.

My students were simply required to share their project on Pitch Day. They planned it out, and Pitch Day was time to share their plan. There are specific things that must be discussed during pitches, including all of the things that were included on the Genius Hour Planning Form. However, I chose not specify how my students needed to share these things with the class. If they wished to share by creating an iMovie trailer rather than talking in front of the class, that was fine with me. If they preferred to stand up and just present in the form of a conversation, that was great too.

To introduce the concept of pitching to students, consider sharing video clips from the television show *Shark Tank*, a reality show where aspiring entrepreneurs share their project ideas with potential investors. Many clips are available on YouTube; some of the most effective pitches can be found if you search "best pitches on

Shark Tank." You can even find pitches given by kids by searching "kid pitches on *Shark Tank."* If your students need more guidance when developing their pitches, consider providing them with a simple checklist (see Figure 5). Ideally, pitches should include students' potential project titles and their KWH—what they already know, what they want to know, and how they are going to find out more. They should also share why they chose their project, how their peers can support them, and what they hope to create.

Presenting Pitches

There are several tools that students can use to prepare their pitch to share with the class. Many of my students preferred PowToon (https://www.powtoon.com), which is a platform that allows students to create animated slideshows. Google Slides (https://www.google.com/slides/about) is another way that students can share their pitch with the class. Google Slides is very simple and clean, making it easy for students to create a presentation in a short amount of time. I recently discovered an app called Vidra (http://tentouchapps.com/vidra). This is a great way for younger students to create simple presentations. Voiceovers and images can be added to make the presentation engaging and students love the simplicity of the app. Before students present, ensure that each student knows how he or she will deliver his or her presentation. See Figure 6 for an example student pitch handout. Remind students that their pitches only need to be about 3–5 minutes long. This should be just enough time for them to share the necessary information about their project, convince their classmates of their project's benefits, and discuss what they hope to accomplish.

After a student has pitched the project, it's time to hear the feedback from the rest of the class. This is when the community

---

Student Name: _____ Date: _____

Pitch Checklist

Directions: Please include the following information when presenting your pitch to your peers. You will have 3–5 minutes to share the following information.

- ☐ Project Title
- ☐ KWH
    - ☐ K—What do you already know about this project, concept, or idea?
    - ☐ W—What do you want to know about the project, concept, or idea?
    - ☐ H—How are you going to find out what you would like to know about this topic?

- ☐ Why did you choose this project?
- ☐ How can your peers support you as you work on your project?
- ☐ What do you hope to create as a product to represent your project?
- ☐ Other things to consider:
    - ☐ Props—What props will you use, if any, during your pitch?
    - ☐ Technology—What technology will you need to deliver your pitch?

Figure 5. Sample student pitch checklist handout.

---

building comes in and becomes really evident. I love to see collaboration in my classroom, so Pitch Day is a special treat. Students may offer any advice, suggestions, and ideas as long as it's done in a way that is productive and constructive. They may not say things such as, "That's a terrible idea, and it will never work." Instead, they can say, "Your idea is really interesting, but I worry that you might have trouble finding an outside expert. Have you thought of what you might do if this is a problem?"

Student Name:_____ Date:_____

Pitch Form

1. Project Title:_____

2. K—What do you already know?

   _____

   _____

   _____

3. W—What do you want to know?

   _____

   _____

   _____

4. H—How are you going to find out?

   _____

   _____

   _____

5. Will you need any props for your pitch?
   ☐ Yes _____
   ☐ No

6. What will you use to create your pitch presentation? (Check one.)
   ☐ Powtoon   ☐ Vidra   ☐ Google Slides   ☐ iMovie
   ☐ Other _____

   Other technology that you will need for your pitch:_____

   _____

   _____

   _____

Figure 6. Sample student pitch form.

After a student presents a pitch, some questions that might be asked might include:

- Why is this project important to you?

- How do you plan on sharing your project with the world?

- What if your idea doesn't go as planned?

- What can we do to help you carry out your project idea?

- How did you come up with your idea?

These are just a few suggestions, but allowing students to collaborate and discuss project ideas is the goal. Give them the opportunity to really gain interest in the ideas of their peers. Encourage them to become invested in other projects, as this will only build classroom community throughout the process.

The pitch process is so valuable for our students. They begin to see each other differently and realize that they each have different strengths and weaknesses. In doing so, they understand who might be best to collaborate with inside the classroom as they work toward their goals. Understanding that we are in this together is an important part of culture building in the classroom and makes the Genius Hour process much more enjoyable.

Reflection Questions

1. What is the culture like in your own class-room? Do students know each other's strengths and weaknesses?

2. What would Pitch Day look like in your classroom?

3. Do you believe collaboration is natural or does it need to be taught? Do you think there is a difference between collaboration and group work?

4. Are you currently encouraging group work or collaboration in your own classroom?

PITCH

Quick Tips for Implementation

1. Help students understand the difference between collaboration and group work.

2. Share a Shark Tank pitch video (available on YouTube) with students so that they can understand what a pitch might look like.

3. Encourage collaboration and questions during the pitch to build community.

The Technology to Make It Happen

Google Slides
https://www.google.com/slides/about

PowToon
https://www.powtoon.com

Scratch
https://scratch.mit.edu

Vidra
http://tentouchapps.com/vidra

YouTube
https://www.youtube.com

Chapter 6

Project
Igniting the Flame

BIG IDEA

Learning by doing is so much more powerful than learning by worksheet.

When students reach the fourth P—project—of Genius Hour, they are ready to get to work. The fire has been built, the spark has found, and it's time to ignite the flame. They have made plans, shared their idea with their peers, and should be excited about actually carrying the project out. This is when ideas become reality, plans should be carried out, and you should begin to see their passion truly ignite.

Acquiring Materials

Students will need different materials for different projects. Many of them will need access to technology, while others will need tools like a sewing machine, art supplies, or recycled materials. As you begin to ready your room for Genius Hour, don't hesitate to ask others for help. Send a letter home to parents with a list of the things that students need. Ask local businesses if they would be willing to donate items. Many things that students need may not already be in your classroom but can easily be found and added. In doing so, you make Genius Hour a time to focus on learning instead of worrying about getting what students need to complete their projects.

As you collect materials, consider creating a makerspace or keeping a cart in the classroom where you can store materials that students can use to create products. Makerspaces are designed to have a ton of materials that students can work with to create, make, and design. Collecting recyclables for this purpose is a low-cost solution to purchasing miscellaneous project materials. These materials are often things that would be thrown away if not used in a project. If you and your students work together to collect materials throughout the year, you might find that you begin with a maker cart and end up with a full-blown makerspace in no time.

If you find yourself struggling to acquire funds for project materials, DonorsChoose.org (https://www.donorschoose.org) is a wonderful organization that gives teachers an opportunity to write requests for funding for materials they need in the classroom. I have written many DonorsChoose.org requests, and all of them were fully funded. If you begin to notice that there are specific things that your students often need or technology that you would like to have to make Genius Hour meaningful, this is a perfect resource. The key to a successful project on DonorsChoose.org is spreading the word. After creating your request, spread the word like wildfire. Share it on social media, in your school newspaper, and with anyone that will listen. Don't assume that you won't receive funding. I can assure you that if you are willing to ask, someone is willing to listen.

Project Research

Research is something that many teachers ask about when addressing the Genius Hour process. How much research is required? Should I make every student research before beginning their project? Do we need to learn about research before starting Genius Hour?

According to Paul Solarz, fifth-grade teacher and author of *Learn Like a Pirate*, research will happen naturally in the Genius Hour process (P. Solarz, personal communication, January 2017). Students will have to gather information, find out how to do things, and ask questions before moving forward. Research does not have to be the focus of Genius Hour. I agree that it will naturally be a part of the process, and efficient research methods can be introduced throughout the process through mini-lessons and other activities. Students need to be taught how to know if a source is reliable, how to cite sources, and why research is important. The key to this being meaningful is letting it happen when it's appropriate in the process for each project and finding teachable moments that relate to the project.

A great source for mini-lessons on research is ReadWriteThink. Consider lessons by Lisa Storm Fink, such as "Research Building Blocks: 'Organize This!'" (http://www.readwritethink.org/classroom-resources/lesson-plans/research-building-blocks-organize-179.html) and "Research Building Blocks: Examining Electronic Sources" (http://www.readwritethink.org/classroom-resources/lesson-plans/research-building-blocks-examining-149.html).

Meeting With Outside Experts

As students work on their projects, they will begin to meet with their outside experts. This can be done virtually, by phone call, or in person. There are a few specific procedures that I implemented with my students for outside expert meetings. First, we never asked the expert for more than 30 minutes of his or her time. It is important to be respectful and realize that he or she is probably busy and asking for more than that might be unrealistic.

Because we only have 30 minutes, I asked my students to prepare 10 questions for their expert in order of priority. In other words, if there is a question that is really important, it should be toward the top of the list because there is a possibility that there will not be time to ask all of the questions that have been prepared. When preparing the questions, it is important to ask questions that will give them the information that they need to move forward with their project goals. Asking questions that can simply be answered with a yes or a no will not work. I usually started the conversation by asking the student to share some information about his or her project and then asking the expert to share a little bit about what

- What is your favorite thing about your job?
- What education did you receive before becoming a/an _____?
- Do you have any suggestions that would help me carry out my project?
- What role does passion play in your job?
- Which of the 4 C's—collaboration, communication, creativity, and critical thinking—do you use the most in your job and how?
- What was your favorite subject in school?
- What was your least favorite subject in school?
- Have you experienced failure in your job, and how did you overcome that failure?
- How has your job changed over time?
- What is something I can do now to start preparing for a job as a/an _____?

Figure 7. Sample expert interview questions.

he or she does each day. Figure 7 includes some sample interview questions.

Students are also encouraged to ask specific questions pertaining to their projects. Knowing that they only get 10 questions and might not get to all of them gives them an opportunity to prioritize and make decisions about what they will and will not ask.

When meeting with an expert, I always make it a priority to ask how he or she uses some of the standards in their jobs each day. When a student is finished with the questions, I simply ask the expert if he or she can share some specific ways that he or she uses math, science, reading, and writing in his or her daily work. Many times this information is shared throughout the conversation. This helps students make a connection and realize that the standards that they are learning can be connected to the real world.

Building Communication Skills

Because I had my students work on communication skills when talking with an outside expert, my students were not allowed to take notes while speaking to the expert. Instead, I asked them to work on skills like eye contact, nonverbal cues, and listening.

Communication Skills

- ① Eye Contact

- ① Nonverbal Cues

- ① Listening

Let's be real. This generation of students does not communicate well. Because they use their phones for the majority of their communication, their skills are lacking. Eye contact becomes more comfortable as it is practiced. As students are engaged in conversation, it is important that they are practicing these skills and making it a priority to look at who is speaking and offer nonverbal cues to show that they are listening.

Gifted students, especially, often times struggle with really listening. They hear when someone is speaking but have learned that they often already know what is being shared. Because of this, they will "tune out" what is being said and begin thinking about other things that are more engaging or important to them. We can all be guilty of this—many times we are thinking about what we are going to say or how we are going to respond rather than really listening to what is being said. Talking with an outside expert is the perfect opportunity to practice purposeful listening to understand rather than to respond.

Because I wanted students to work on these skills while talking to the experts, I video recorded the conversation for them to refer back to later for information and reflection purposes. This can be done using an iPad, smartphone, or video recorder. While speaking with the expert, students are making eye contact, using nonverbal cues, and listening. When it is time to take notes or get information that they need from the interview, students can watch the video with the ability to pause or fast forward to get what they need.

Field Trips to Meet Outside Experts

There were a few times that I actually took students on personal field trips to visit outside experts. If the expert was local and I was able to work it out with the parents, I took students on a personal field trip. There was an Arabian horse farm right up the road from our school. One of my students absolutely loved horses, and she wanted to learn more. I simply called the horse farm, asked if we could visit, and then set it up so that her mom could come as well. After school one day, we met at the farm and she was able to get all of the information that she needed. The same rules applied as she talked to the expert. I still wanted her to work on communication skills, so I documented the visit with an iPad throughout the time that we were there (see Figure 8).

I had another student who was interested in the culinary arts. Our school was also fairly close to a technical college, so I called the culinary arts department and asked if we could visit. They were more than happy to not only let us visit but offered us a complete tour with a question-answer opportunity. We were able to spend a morning on the college campus touring the culinary arts school and asking questions (see Figure 9). It was very inspiring to see my student as she got to actually experience what a future in the culinary arts world might look like.

Figure 8. A student visits an Arabian horse farm to learn more from her outside expert.

Talking with an outside expert
is the perfect opportunity to
practice purposeful listening to
understand rather than to respond.

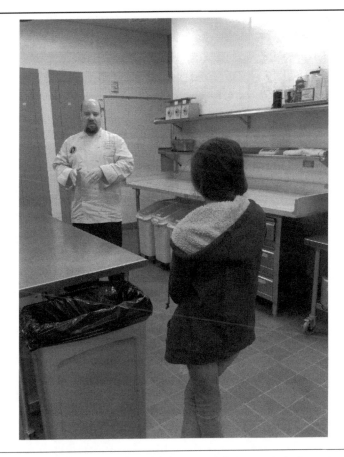

Figure 9. A student speaks with her outside expert during a tour of a local culinary arts school.

A Meaningful Outside Expert Interview

My favorite expert experience was when one of my third-grade students asked me if SeaWorld could be her outside expert. She was writing a digital book about dolphins and really wanted to talk to a dolphin trainer. I was almost positive that I wasn't going to be able to make that happen, but I had to try. I contacted SeaWorld and waited anxiously for their reply. That same day, I received an e-mail, and they explained that they would be more than happy to meet with my student and share any information that she might need to complete her project.

I set up a Skype session, and within a couple of weeks my student was able to virtually meet with the trainer. Not only did the dolphin trainer offer amazing information, but she also took her iPad out to Dolphin Cove, and we were able to see a real dolphin (see Figure 10). As my student asked questions, the trainer instructed the dolphin to do what was needed to answer her questions. If we needed to see dolphin's teeth, the trainer fed the dolphin a fish and zoomed into the mouth. If my student wanted to know how fast the dolphin could swim, the trainer instructed him to swim across the water. This experience was so much more meaningful than me pretending to know something that I did not. Hearing the trainer explain how she uses math, science, and technology in her job each day had such an impact on the student and resulted in a meaningful learning experience.

> Finding an expert can often take a project to the next level and give students the motivation that they need to carry it out.

Outside experts are a powerful piece to the Genius Hour process. As teachers, many of us feel guilty when we cannot answer a specific question or give students the information that they need to get a correct answer. Genius Hour will not allow you to have all of the answers. I am not a dolphin trainer, nor am I an accredited chef. Although I can't give my students information about those subjects

Figure 10. A student Skypes with a SeaWorld dolphin trainer.

that might be meaningful to them, I can design a learning experience that will.

Although it might not always be easy, finding an expert can often take a project to the next level and give students the motivation that they need to carry it out. As education changes and technology advances, it is important that we move away from writing specific lesson plans about giving information and move toward facilitating meaningful learning experiences. Outside expert experiences give us an opportunity to do this in the classroom and help our students make connections that might not otherwise be made.

Student Accountability and Meeting Standards

As students work on their projects, they should be held accountable for what they accomplish each day. Because every student is working on a different project, it will be difficult for you to monitor every student every day. Giving students ownership of their learning is one of the many benefits of Genius Hour and helps them realize that learning is happening each time they work on their project. In order to track my students' learning, we used Trello (https://trello.com) and KidBlog (http://kidblog.org).

Because many administrators will want to know how Genius Hour addresses the standards, having students' Trello boards, or another documentation strategy that can be shared, is very beneficial.

Documenting the Standards Met

Trello boards are set up while planning (see Chapter 4), and we began to use them when students started working on their projects.

At the end of each Genius Hour, I required my students to update their Trello boards. With this tool, students can share the standards that were addressed each day in their work by adding a "card" to the specific list. For example, if a student used measurement to measure fabric for his or her project, he or she would document that under a math list on a Trello board. If he or she read a blog and did something with that information, he or she might list reading comprehension under a English language arts list. This gives students an opportunity to realize that they are learning through application. It helps them understand that learning doesn't just happen by completing a worksheet, but is instead happening all of the time.

Because many administrators will want to know how Genius Hour addresses the standards, having students' Trello boards, or another documentation strategy that can be shared, is very beneficial. (*Note.* See Chapter 10 for a section on talking to administrators about Genius Hour.) Whichever strategy you use is evidence of the learning that is taking place and proof that students are accomplishing so much more that just making, researching, and doing. Students begin to see how their learning applies to real life. They make connections that cannot be made by completing a worksheet and do things that will be remembered for years to come instead of just on the test the next week.

Challenging Students to Apply the Standards

Bringing the standards into Genius Hour can be very powerful and can help students see them differently. I often gave my students three or four standards at the beginning of a week. I wrote them on the board and challenged students to use them during Genius Hour time. I provided one standard for each subject area and asked students to be creative. I was often surprised at the many ways that they found to practice a specific standard or skill within their projects. Minecraft projects became opportunities to practice area and perimeter; making a dog collar became an opportunity to practice writing, as students prepared a presentation for the school board to share what they had learned and which standards they had addressed; and sewing projects became opportunities to learn more about measurement and fractions. I could go on—but you get the idea.

The Importance of Asking Specific Questions

The standards can also be addressed through asking specific questions. As students are working on their projects, be aware of opportunities to weave the standards into what they are doing. As you walk around and supervise, stop and ask them questions that will make them aware of what they are learning. Students may not realize that as they are correcting their blog post, they are practicing their editing and grammar skills. A student that is creating an outdoor garden may not realize that he or she is learning about ecosystems as he or she designs a living space for specific plants and insects. However, by questioning and helping students make those connections, they begin to see the standards come to life.

Blogging

Updating Trello boards often takes no longer than 5–10 minutes. Afterward, I asked my students to reflect on their learning for the day by blogging about their experiences. I did this for many reasons. I believe that blogging is a skill that students need to learn. Blogging encourages writing and helps students understand that writing has many purposes. Blogging also gives students an opportunity to write for an authentic audience, as blog posts can be shared and made public. It is so important to share blogs and not keep them in the walls of your classroom. If blogs aren't shared, students may not understand the purpose or meaning in writing. However, when they are shared, they begin to see that others are interested in their ideas and have suggestions that can be helpful as they work through their projects.

> Blogging encourages writing and helps students understand that writing has many purposes.

Blogging Platforms

In my classroom, we used a platform called KidBlog to write our blogs. Although KidBlog is not free, it is a great option for blogging in the classroom because of the safety features. If blogs are going to be shared, you should be in control of what the students see and the comments that they receive, especially in an elementary classroom. Using KidBlog gives you the ability to moderate comments. In other words, if a student receives an inappropriate comment on his or her blog, you can delete that comment before he or she ever has access. This gives students a safe space to practice blogging skills and assures parents that the teacher will always be in control.

Secondary teachers might use blogging platforms such as WordPress (https://wordpress.com), Blogger (https://www.blogger.com), or Weebly (https://www.weebly.com). Weebly for Education (https://education.weebly.com) is a great option as it allows teachers to create an account and add student accounts. This allows the teacher to have access to the accounts but gives students the freedom to manage and post when appropriate. I believe that digital citizenship must be a priority when students are sharing with an authentic audience. Students must have boundaries and teachers should monitor closely. However, if done correctly, this is a powerful piece that allows students to be transparent and learn how and why to share their successes and failures.

Encouraging High-Level Reflection

As my students began to blog to reflect on their learning, I realized that my students were simply remembering what they did each day. Throughout their blogs, I read sentences like, "Today I . . ." and they merely went on to list what they did that day. Although remembering is important, this is the lowest level in the taxonomy of reflection (Pappas, 2010). I wanted my students to reflect by creating and evaluating and in doing so, understand why reflection is so powerful.

In looking for ways for my students to understand reflection, I found Tony Vincent's Reflection QR Codes (2013). QR codes, or quick response codes, are simple images that can be scanned with a device, such as a smartphone or tablet, to obtain information. To scan a code, you need an app such as QR Code Reader for iPhone or Android. You simply open the app, which accesses your device's camera. You then point the camera at the code you're intending to scan, and it directs you to, in this case, the URL embedded in the code. Vincent's Reflection QR Codes direct to randomly generated reflection questions, such as:

- When something got hard, what did you do to help yourself?

- If you were the teacher, what comments would you make about yourself?

ⓘ How much did you know about the subject before we started?

See Figure 11 to use your smartphone to try one of his QR codes for yourself, or simply visit http://tonyv.me/reflect.

If QR codes are not an option for you because of a lack of devices, you could write reflection questions on index cards or strips of paper and have students draw from a cup or jar. You could also simply display random questions on the board or projector at the end of class each day. Using a tool like Google Slides or PowerPoint, you could even create slides with questions to use throughout the year. Blogging is also not the only option available when students are asked to reflect and respond to higher level questions. Students could discuss in pairs or write their responses in a journal. You could also select a few students to share their thoughts with the class. Pappas (2010) and many other online resources can provide you with more direction as you begin developing questions. Some reflection questions to get you started might include:

ⓘ How can you use what you learned today outside of school?

ⓘ What did you learn about yourself today?

ⓘ How would you explain this topic to someone else?

ⓘ How can you apply what you've learned to another subject or class?

ⓘ What did you find most engaging about today's lesson?

Figure 11. Reflection question QR code. From "Reflection Facilitated by QR Codes" by T. Vincent, 2013, *Learning in Hand*, retrieved from http://learninginhand.com/blog/2013/7/5/roll-reflect-with-qr-codes. Copyright 2013 by T. Vincent. Reprinted with permission.

Seeing Students Improve

I absolutely loved the idea of students having quick access to reflection questions that would deepen their thinking and encourage higher level reflection. As my students began to use the QR codes and respond to higher level questions, their writing changed. Higher level thinking questions made reflection a reality in my classroom. The more we used them, the more my students began to understand the purpose of reflection and became comfortable with sharing their learning. They no longer just remembered what they did each day, but they thought ahead and began to evaluate their own work. Below is an example of a student's blog post at the beginning of the year:

I was really happy that a lot of the supplies we needed was right in the classroom. My partner and I got a lot more accomplished then I thought we would! We have a lot of the items that we need. I think that our project will go really fast! I was really satisfied that we got so much done.

Here's a blog post from the same student toward the middle of the school year after using the QR codes for some time:

I have gotten a lot better at deciding which toys we need to throw away, maybe because we have a lot that were good, and not very many that were bad. It is a lot easier to make the toys. I think that I've gotten better using Pinterest and pinning things. I think that next time, I will make more of the braiding toys and try some of the really cool toys that people made on Pinterest. I personally think that I did pretty well today. We checked all of our toys and sorted through the toys that are safe and the toys that we are going to throw away or improve. It is really important to me that the toys are totally safe, so that takes a lot of improving and testing then improving and testing again. I have gotten a whole lot better at communicating with my partner. We came up with a lot of really good ideas for toys, some are based off of something else and some aren't based off anything but our minds. I really like doing Genius Hour because we get to pick whatever we want to do or our passion and take it however far we want and make it as big as we want it to be. Like if we want it to last a whole year, we can make it last a whole year. But we do have to finish what we start. It is really easy to finish what you start in Genius Hour because, like I said before it is what you choose and it is your passion, whatever that is. It is so much fun being in GT, because it is like your free time. I think that every school needs a GT or an hour or five to work on a project that can change the world, hopefully for the better. That is my super long post, hope you liked it.

Understanding why we blog and what reflection is all about made a huge difference. The second post is written with purpose. She is not simply remembering, but instead reflecting on and evaluating her experience that day.

Remembering is what the learner did and how. Reflection is what the learner learned and why.

As my students continued to respond to higher level reflection questions, their writing continued to improve. Reflection is a skill that students need and even a skill that we as teachers should use during our own practice. Reflection brings clarity, perspective, and understanding. Without reflection, learning will not stick and meaning cannot be found in what has been done. Remembering is what the learner did and how. Reflection is what the learner learned and why. In order for learning to be meaningful, we must begin to focus on reflection instead of remembering.

Using Digital Portfolios

Although blogging is a very powerful tool and a simple way to share student reflections, many teachers prefer portfolios. Digital portfolios are a great option and a wonderful way for students to document their learning and reflection as they work on their projects.

I recently learned of a digital portfolio option called FreshGrade (https://www.freshgrade.com). I couldn't help but see how this platform could be beneficial for students working on a Genius Hour project. With FreshGrade, students can upload photos, short video clips, audio, and documents. This a free tool that offers paid features as well. Students can then reflect on their work as well as receive feedback from the teacher and others that have access to their portfolios. I believe that feedback is so much more powerful than grades, and with digital portfolios like FreshGrade, making feedback the priority is possible. Portfolios, however, can be used as an assessment tool. (*Note.* See Chapter 10 for a section on assessment.)

Many elementary teachers are uncomfortable allowing their students to share their blogs on social media and need an option in between. Digital portfolios are a perfect fit and are very simple to use. Just like blogs, digital portfolios can be accessed from anywhere at any time and make documentation and reflection very convenient for everyone involved.

In closing, the project portion of Genius Hour can be the most chaotic, simply because everyone is doing something different and asking different questions. It's important to realize that you must become a facilitator and let go of needing to know the answers to every question they might have. Instead of providing answers, help them find answers. Learn with them and don't be afraid to say, "I don't know." Learning with your students will make your job much more fun and will help them realize that you are all in this together. So, sit back, enjoy the ride, and appreciate the opportunity to grow as a learner yourself, as you watch their passions and ideas come alive.

Reflection Questions

1. How do you feel about feedback? Is this a priority in your classroom? If not, what can you do to make it a priority?

2. Do your students know how to reflect, or do they know how to remember? What are some ways that you can give your students opportunities to reflect?

3. How comfortable are you with not having all of the answers? Will you be okay with saying "I don't know" and learning with your students?

PROJECT

Quick Tips for Implementation

1. Gather materials by asking for materials from home or getting donations.

2. Set up appointments with outside experts and discuss requirements for the interviews.

3. Weave the standards into the projects by supervising and asking questions as students work on their projects.

4. After Genius Hour, give students an opportunity to reflect and document their learning.

The Technology to Make It Happen

Blogger
https://www.blogger.com

DonorsChoose.org
https://donorschoose.org

FreshGrade
https://www.freshgrade.com

Google Hangouts
https://hangouts.google.com

PROJECT

Continued

KidBlog
http://kidblog.org

Reflection QR Codes
http://learninginhand.com/blog/2013/7/5/roll-reflect-with-qr-codes

Skype
https://www.skype.com

Trello
https://trello.com

Weebly
https://www.weebly.com

Weebly for Education
https://education.weebly.com

WordPress
https://wordpress.com

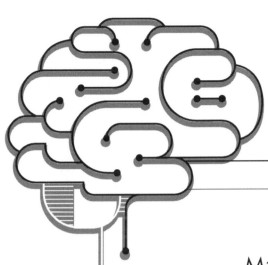

Chapter 7

Product

Making the S'mores

BIG IDEA

"If students are sharing their work, they want it to be good. If they are sharing it with you they just want it to be good enough."
—Rushton Hurley

Just like s'mores, Genius Hour projects are made to be shared. It's no fun if students complete a project and have nothing to show for it. We want them to have proof of their work, something to represent the project that they've done. Making s'mores can be very messy, but once they are done and you taste the goodness of what was created, they are worth the time and mess. Genius Hour products should be the same way.

I had students develop incredible projects, including

- a backyard classroom, where they designed and created a space for students to learn, read, and create outdoors (see Figure 12);

- blankets for babies, where they learned to sew by making baby blankets (see Figure 13);

- a super collar, where they created a dog collar with a remote to alert the dog when a car is coming (see Figure 14); and

- ice cream creations, where they created and made new ice cream flavors to submit to Blue Bell Creameries for consideration (see Figure 15).

No matter what students create, the process might be messy and time consuming, but the product should be well worth the effort.

Time Constraints and Completing Projects

Finishing a project is sometimes a difficult task. Students do not necessarily know what determines a project being complete and sometimes aren't sure when to say that they are done. I eventually

Figure 12. Students create an outdoor classroom for their Genius Hour project.

chose not give my students a timeline as they worked toward completing their projects. In years past, students were to complete a project a semester. This caused several problems. One problem was that students would finish quickly and then have too much time to be off task. Another was that students would need longer than a semester to complete their projects so they ended up with incomplete projects that never resulted in a product.

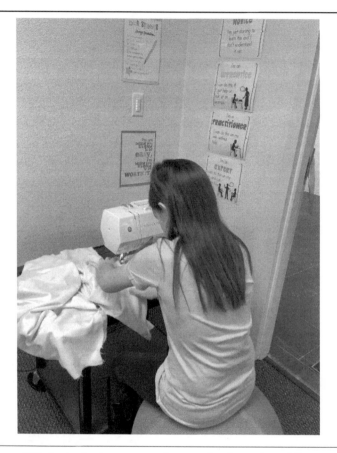

Figure 13. A student uses newly acquired sewing skills to make baby blankets.

Because of this, I stopped dictating how much time a project should or should not take. Instead, I allowed students to determine how long it should take and make changes to that timeline as they work. As long as they were on task and working toward their goal, a specific date was not necessarily important. One project might take 3 weeks, while another takes all year—it doesn't matter. The goal is to work toward a completed product.

Figure 14. Students use electronic building blocks, littleBits, to develop a high-tech dog collar.

If there is a need for a time limit or your students need specific time constraints, consider setting those time limits together as a class. Ask your students for feedback and set a limit that is realistic and attainable. It might be a good idea to put together a detailed timeline so that students stay on track and know what needs to be done when. Although things might not go exactly as planned, students will be able to make adjustments throughout the timeline to ensure completion by a specific date.

Figure 15. Students meet with a Blue Bell Creameries representative to taste ice cream flavors.

Sharing Students' Work

A *product* is something that represents the project and can be shared out with the world. Some examples might include scarves that were made for the homeless, a video game created on Scratch, a video of a model volcano, or a digital book written on Book Creator (http://bookcreator.com) about wolves. Although digital projects can be shared very easily, physical models and paper projects can be shared as well. It might require more creativity and time, but sharing the project is an important part of the Genius Hour process.

If students are not going to share their work with anyone, what is the point?

Finding Authentic Audiences

An authentic audience is an important piece to the Genius Hour puzzle. If students are not going to share their work with anyone, what is the point? What is the goal? An audience brings the possibility of exposure and real-world connections. When student work is shared, ideas are given worth and students begin to realize that their ideas have the potential to change the world. I am not suggesting that you take a picture of a worksheet and share it on social media. But if it is a project that might be valuable to others, it's important to share.

While planning, students should have decided who their audience will be (see Chapter 4). If the project is a video game, they might want to share it with a community of gamers to offer feedback and advice. I had two students that created a dog collar using littleBits (http://littlebits.cc), a series of electronic building blocks. The collar was interactive, and the owner could use a remote to warn the dog when they were in danger. It was such a great idea, and they worked really hard to make their idea a reality. When we shared the collar on Twitter, we included Twitter handles for PetSmart and Petco because we knew they might be interested in what was created. Finding the right audience might result in contact, internships, and even possible patents or inventions.

Many teachers ask how projects should be shared. Social media—including Facebook, Twitter, Instagram, etc.—is a powerful tool and, when used appropriately, can be a great way to promote student work. This is a great way for students to begin to realize the positive impact social media can have when it is used for the right reasons. For high school students, this can be done using their own accounts. For elementary and middle school students, teachers should consider creating educational accounts to use for this purpose.

The Importance of Sharing

Student work can also be shared on a school website, at educational conferences, or in parent newsletters. Any opportunity that gives students a chance to have their work seen should be taken advantage of. Rushton Hurley said, "If students are sharing their work with the world, they want it to be good. If they're just sharing it with you, they want it to be good enough."

Think about that for a second. How often do students go above and beyond on a worksheet that is completed for the teacher? How many times will they edit a YouTube video before posting it online? Knowing that something will be shared with the world brings meaning and relevance to students' work. They are familiar with audiences and creating things for one person is no longer relevant to them.

> Knowing that something will be shared with the world brings meaning and relevance to students' work.

I often share the story of my own children and their determination to "get it right" when it's going to be shared. A while back, we were coming home from a baseball tournament and our two youngest children were making a video to share online. They recorded the video over and over, probably six or seven times, before they felt like it was ready to post for everyone to see. However, that evening when we got home and it was homework time, they completed their math worksheets and threw them back in their binders without giving them a second look. Why? Because it wasn't something that they felt represented them. They knew what the teacher wanted and knew what needed to be done to get the grade that they wanted. They also knew that no one else was going to see their work. The teacher would look it over, put a red grade at the top, and it might be counted toward their final grade.

So, what's the difference? The audience. Students take pride in work that will be shared out with an audience. Realizing that someone could see their work and take interest is a powerful incentive to be mindful and purposeful.

Sharing Work Safely

In order to share work safely, I have several rules. Most importantly, students do not share last names and they do not share the school district name. Digital citizenship is no longer optional in education. Students are always sharing things on social media and talking to strangers online. Whether or not that makes us uncomfortable no longer matters. It's not fair to be frustrated when they do dangerous things online because they have not been taught otherwise. We can complain about their digital citizenship, but that won't change things. But giving them an opportunity to practice online skills in a safe environment will.

Figure 16 includes some rules for sharing work online safely. Teaching students about online safety is all about conversation. Discuss these rules—or your own—for sharing work online early in and throughout the Genius Hour process. Talk to your students,

Student Name:_____ Date:_____

Rules for Sharing Work Online

1. Share first names only.
2. Never mention where you live or where you go to school.
3. Always ask permission before sharing.
4. Be willing to accept feedback and suggestions.
5. Never engage in conversation without adult supervision.
6. Use social media to share positive information.
7. Think about the consequences before sharing anything online.
8. Know your audience and remember that your work will be shared.
9. Talk to an adult if you see or receive anything inappropriate online.
10. Don't post pictures of friends or family members without permission.

Figure 16. Sample online safety rules handout.

and be honest. Listen to their concerns, and don't overreact when they share their real-life experiences. Some students will be more aware of unsafe online behaviors than others. No matter what, it's important to use every opportunity that you can to share the importance of safety and self-control when sharing anything online.

We should not be scared to share student work. We should be scared not to. If we are keeping all of the work our students do within the four walls of the classroom, who is benefiting from what has been done? Whom are our students impacting? How can they inspire change? Our students have amazing ideas, innovative minds, and creative skills. Transparency in the classroom gives them the ability to share themselves, and because of technology, this is very easy to achieve.

Don't Forget About Creativity

Give students an opportunity to be creative with their products. Don't be judgmental or afraid to share because it's not what you would have done. Creativity is something that should be encouraged and students should feel free to create products that they feel represent their learning. Although it's easy to feel like what is shared represents you and your classroom, try to understand that a Genius Hour project is very personal, and the product may not be what we would have imagined. That's okay. As long as the product can be explained and represents the student's goals and learning, it is acceptable.

Reflection Questions

1. How do you feel about an authentic audience? Are you comfortable sharing student work on social media?

2. What are some specific ways that you can share student products?

3. How transparent is your classroom? What can you do to become more transparent?

4. How difficult will it be to let student work be authentic and creative without trying to control the products before they are shared?

PRODUCT

Quick Tips for Implementation

1. Decide whether you will give a time limit for product completion.

2. Encourage students to create products that can be shared.

3. Discuss the importance of transparency and why work should be shared with an authentic audience.

4. Teach students the rules for sharing work safely and appropriately online.

The Technology to Make It Happen

Book Creator
http://bookcreator.com

Facebook
https://www.facebook.com

Instagram
https://www.instagram.com

littleBits
http://littlebits.cc

Twitter
https://twitter.com

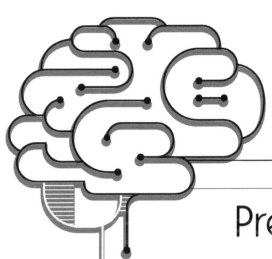

Chapter 8

Presentation

Watching It Burn

BIG IDEA

Keep the end goal in mind. If the goal is to present what has been learned, don't try to control how that is done.

Have you ever made something or accomplished something and couldn't wait to tell someone? This is how students should feel as they begin to complete their Genius Hour projects. They should be excited and proud of what they have created, designed, learned, and achieved. Just like a well-built campfire that can be enjoyed, a successful Genius Hour project results in a presentation that is fun to watch.

Wrapping Up

Students should always still have questions when the project is done.

When the project is completed, it is time for students to complete their LAQ (see Chapter 4). L stands for what I learned, A stands for what action I took, and Q stands for what questions I still have. They might have learned things about themselves as well as information about a specific topic. In doing so, they begin to see themselves as learners and begin to realize what works for them and what doesn't. The action that they take simply depends on the project. This is very closely related to the product. The product is a direct result of the action that they took. For example, the action might be, "I used a sewing machine to make pillowcases for children who are in the hospital and delivered them over Spring Break."

Students should always still have questions when the project is done. It's possible that they have may have more questions than when they started. This enables them to see that learning never stops. My students documented their responses on their Trello boards under the KWHLAQ list. This strategy kept everything together and allowed us to document all of the learning in one place.

Managing Presentations

Presentations can be difficult simply because everyone will be presenting at a different time if you do not put time restrictions on the projects. Keeping up with when students are ready to present can be quite a task. However, encouraging students to take ownership and simply sign up for presentation times can make this easier on everyone.

Providing Choice

Presenting any type of project can be very stressful for students. Many students do not enjoy standing up and speaking in front of their peers. Although most will be excited to share, this part of the project also has the potential to cause anxiety and fear. Because of this, it is important to do all that we can as teachers to allow them choice as they decide how they will present. I always try to focus on the end goal. If the goal is to share the information that they have learned throughout the project, why do I care what platform they use to do so?

Provide students with choices when it comes to creating presentations. Introduce them to tools such as:

- Google Slides (https://slides.google.com),

- iMovie (http://www.apple.com/imovie),

- Powtoon (https://www.powtoon.com),

① Prezi (https://prezi.com), and

① Vidra (http://tentouchapps.com/vidra).

Providing students choice is beneficial for both you and them. It encourages creativity and sends the message that you trust them to make a decision. I always like to encourage teachers to think about the goal of the assignment. If the goal is to practice reading comprehension, why do we have to dictate what students read? Will they not be more engaged if they are reading something that they are interested in? The same is true for preparing a presentation. If the end goal is to present what was learned, why do we care what tool the student uses? As long as it includes the information that we have asked them to include, the tool should not matter.

These tools may even be used during the Pitch stage of the project (see Chapter 5, p. 51). Students may want to try something new, and that's a good thing. Let them decide how they will share their work, and support them in the process. Just like the pitch, it's not important what tool they use but how they use it. I often encouraged students to use different tools each time they presented. Using a variety of tools helps them find what works for them as well as helps them stay open to new possibilities.

Planning Presentations

Presentations should only be 3–5 minutes. Throughout the presentation, a student can share any information that he or she would like, but it is essential that he or she shares his or her LAQ. Figure 17 is an example of a form that will help students stay focused and offer ideas for what they may want to share in their presentations, such as their LAQ, information about their product, how they shared their work with an authentic audience, and any roadblocks they had to work through over the course of their project.

Student Name:_____ Date:_____

Presentation Planning

LAQ

L	A	Q
What Did I Learn?	**What Action Did I Take?**	**What Questions Do I Still Have?**

What was your product?

_____

_____

_____

_____

How did you share your work with the world?

_____

_____

_____

_____

Figure 17. Sample student presentation planning handout.

Look back at your potential roadblocks. Were these a problem, and how did you overcome them?

_____

_____

_____

_____

_____

Major Successes	Epic Failures

What did you learn about yourself?

_____

_____

_____

_____

Figure 17. Continued.

The Benefits of Building Public Speaking Skills

By presenting to the class, students are practicing important skills that do not come naturally for most students. For many students, presenting will be awkward and forced at first. They will be nervous, and it may seem very rehearsed. However, as they begin to realize that they are simply sharing their learning with their peers, you might begin to see a shift in their presentation style.

> Speaking in public may not be for everyone, but it is a skill that students must have for the real world.

I remember one student in particular who struggled with her first presentation. She was very anxious, and getting through the presentation was rough. However, after she had spoken in front of the class twice, everything changed. She became comfortable, confident, and realized the power of her own voice. From that moment on, things got better and better, and I ended up telling her parents that I was convinced she had a future in public speaking.

Presentations can be assessed by the teacher, self-assessed by students, or assessed by peers. Should you choose to assess students' presentations, the Buck Institute for Education has a number of easy-to-use rubrics found at https://www.bie.org/objects/cat/rubrics. This is a great resource with a variety of rubrics appropriate for assessing presentations. (*Note.* See Chapter 10 for more information about assessing Genius Hour projects.)

Speaking in public may not be for everyone, but it is a skill that students must have for the real world. Thinking about the future, there are many jobs that require employees to give presentations, share information, and speak before a group. Although it may look different in different organizations, having these skills will most definitely be beneficial and worth the time spent giving classroom presentations.

Reflection Questions

1. Do you give your students choices when they present material to the class?

2. How important is communication? How can you give your students an opportunity to communicate their learning with their peers?

3. Why do you think it is important for students to still have questions even after they have completed the project?

PRESENTATION

Quick Tips for Implementation

1. Explain LAQ (what I learned, what action I took, and what questions I still have) and have students complete a presentation planning form.

2. Ask students to sign up for presentation times.

3. Encourage students to use different tools to present based on what is comfortable for them.

The Technology to Make It Happen

Google Slides
https://slides.google.com

PowToon
https://www.powtoon.com

iMovie
http://www.apple.com/imovie

Vidra
http://tentouchapps.com/vidra

Prezi
https://prezi.com

Everything Else You Need to Know for Genius Hour Success

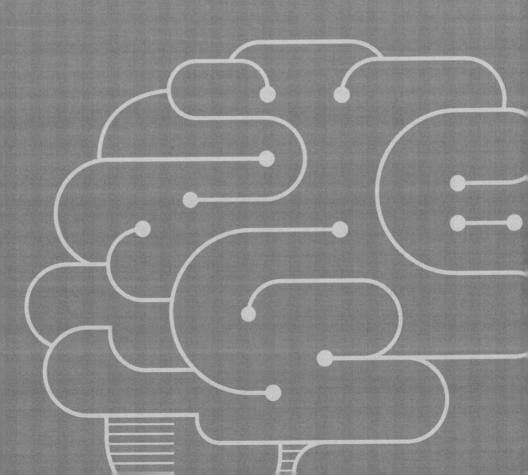

Chapter 9

When the Fire Fizzles

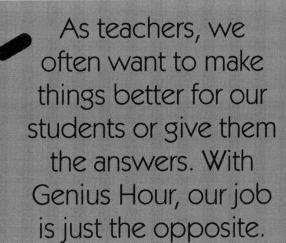

BIG IDEA

As teachers, we often want to make things better for our students or give them the answers. With Genius Hour, our job is just the opposite.

We've all watched a fire go out. Sometimes the fire fizzles slowly over time, and other times it can be extinguished quickly. The same is true for student passions—especially during Genius Hour. Students can slowly lose interest for different reasons or they can quickly become frustrated by circumstances. In this chapter, you'll find strategies for allowing students, particularly gifted students, to experience failure and problem solve on their own, as well as what to do when a project really does fall apart.

Letting Gifted Students Experience Failure

There are so many reasons that Genius Hour is powerful in any classroom. In the gifted classroom especially, there are specific benefits and reasons that this type of learning is just what students need in order prepare for life. Although standards are important and must be taught, we must find ways to connect those standards with real life or they lose their meaning. Gifted students often understand this. If they don't think it is something that they can use, they will not be willing to engage.

Gifted students deserve to experience failure at school.

But, more than that, Genius Hour gives students an opportunity to fail. Some will find this difficult. For many gifted students, failure is not an option. They have breezed through every grade level and every subject. The very thought of failure is inconceivable. Because many gifted students are rarely challenged, they do not know how to deal with anything other than success. Many students do not experience failure until college, and when they do, they do not know how to react or what to do with themselves. Their fear of failure has decreased their willingness to take risks, and as a result, they do not see failure as a learning opportunity. Instead, they see it as a weakness or something that they are not willing to risk.

Gifted students deserve to experience failure at school. This needs to happen in a safe environment that allows them to see that failure does not mean that success is impossible. I often explained to parents that many of the lessons that I planned and Genius Hour in particular, often set their children up to fail. In designing activities that I knew would result in failure, I was able to see how their children handled the situation and help them find ways to handle it more appropriately the next time around. This learning helped my students begin to realize that failure does not define them as a person. Instead, it means that they need to change their way of thinking, make adjustments, or learn more about something before moving on. All of these things result in a true learning experience that will give them the skills that they need to become resilient and willing to take the risks that are often necessary to achieve a goal.

Resist the urge to solve the problem for them or even offer suggestions.

When a student experiences failure or frustration while working on a passion project, it's important not to come in and save the day. As teachers, we often want to make things better for our students or give them the answers. With Genius Hour, our job is just the opposite. Often times, the real learning happens in the struggle, so it's important to let it happen. Provide support and encouragement. Resist the urge to solve the problem for them or even offer suggestions. Instead, ask questions about how they think the problem can be solved:

- What do you think can be done differently?
- Who else can you talk with to get back on track?
- How can you use this setback to make the project even better?

Doing these things lets students know that we trust them and we value their judgment. As adults, we might not always agree with the direction that they choose to go with their solution or even their original ideas when planning the project. However, it's important to let them experience the learning. If the learning is always just happening to them and they aren't experiencing the process by being involved and making decisions, it's meaningless.

Where There's a Will, There's a Way

I remember one day in particular that one of my students was working on her project. She was a very quiet student who typically worked alone. She was very focused and absolutely loved learning about horses. We had taken a personal field trip to a local horse farm, and she had learned so much. For several weeks, she had been working on a website to share her knowledge with others. I looked up one day, and she was jogging toward my desk. Because she was such a quiet student, I knew if she was jogging toward me, there was a problem. She came to me with tears in her eyes and said that she had deleted her website. I explained that it would have been difficult to completely delete the website and assured her that I could find it. Well, it turned out, I was wrong. I couldn't find it anywhere and had to tell her that the website was gone. She was really upset, and it was difficult as her teacher to see her struggle with the fact that her hard work was completely erased. I explained to her that I would do whatever it took to help her as she worked toward a solution. I asked her to think about what would help her the most and just let me know. I felt terrible.

She went back to her table, and I noticed she was very focused on her computer. She was working so hard, and I was encouraged by her motivation and willingness to start over and get right to work—or so I thought. About 15 or 20 minutes later, she came back to my desk and asked me to call a phone number. Puzzled, I asked her whom I was calling and she simply said, "Please call." I felt so badly about what had happened, I thought the least I could do was call the number. As I dialed, I realized I had no idea who I was calling and chuckled when they answered the phone, "Weebly headquarters, how may I help you?" I explained her situation and also explained that I was aware they couldn't fix it but wanted to call because she had asked me to do so. To my surprise, the customer service representative asked for her username and password. Thinking they were playing along, I gave them the information and waited for them to explain that there was nothing that they could do. Instead, she said to have my student log out and log back in. She did so and her website appeared! They explained that it had been restored and thanked us for calling. We thanked them and hung up. My student took her computer back to her desk and continued to work.

My fifth-grade student had used the skills that she gained while working on Genius Hour to fix a problem that I had no idea how to address.

I sat there in disbelief. My fifth-grade student had used the skills that she gained while working on Genius Hour to fix a problem that I had no idea how to address. She knew that I wasn't the end all, be all. She made the choice to spend her time finding another way and because of that choice, she saved herself lots of time and work. I was so proud of her and realized that day that her perseverance and resilience changed the course of her project. It was a good day.

When a Student Loses Interest or a Project Falls Apart

Many times, students decide they do not want to finish a project. They may start out very passionate and excited and then the fire fizzles. It's not as exciting, it might be too challenging, or they may just be over it. It can often take one small obstacle for a student to give up on a project. For example, an outside expert may cancel, or students might not be able to get the supplies that they need. Teachers often ask me if I allow students to switch projects before finishing another. For me, it depended on the student and the situation. If the student was one who had difficulty staying focused and needed to work on staying with one project, then I explained that this was an opportunity for growth and he or she needed to stick it out. However, if the student typically finished things and simply wasn't passionate about what he or she was doing, I would consider the change.

When the passion is lost, Genius Hour loses its purpose. Students should be excited about working on their project and should think about it even outside of the classroom. If these things aren't happening, they aren't truly passionate about what they have chosen to work on. As a teacher, we must ask questions and have conversations to find out if that was because of a challenging situation or just a lack of interest. The decision to switch ideas or drop a project completely should be made together between the teacher and the student after an honest conversation and careful consideration.

It's important not to completely give up on an idea if it is one that will beneficial for your school or others—even if the student with the original idea does not complete it. I once had two students who wanted to create an outdoor classroom for our campus. They came up with several ideas, sketches, and even talked to administration about the idea. However, they were not able to complete the project before moving on to another campus. The next year, I had a couple of students take interest, and then a second-grade teacher heard about our idea. She had a parent in her classroom who was getting her Ph.D. in horticulture. The parent became involved, and the outdoor space became more than we ever imagined it could be. From an idea came an amazing project that now involves all of the grade levels on campus and an amazing space that is beneficial for everyone.

One suggestion is to work on your own Genius Hour project so that your students can see your perseverance and willingness to see things through. Share your struggles with them, and talk to them about what you are experiencing as you go through the process. They will appreciate your willingness to be the lead learner. Your passion may fade; you may struggle and become frustrated. Stay the course, and encourage them to do the same.

Fires fizzle. They don't burn hot without being stoked, fanned, and tended to by someone that has a desire to keep it aflame. The same is true for student's passion. As educators, we may have to ask more questions, offer more resources, take them on a personal field trip, or give them more opportunities to share their passion with others. Fan the flame. Be interested in their interests. In doing so, students begin to realize that their ideas are interesting to others and their passions are worth exploring. Don't get frustrated when you begin to see the fire dying down. Take action and help them find a way to reignite what once burned so bright.

Reflection Questions

1. Are you willing to fail in front of your students? Why or why not?

2. Do you give your students an opportunity to fail safely in your classroom, or is failure always a negative experience?

3. What will you do when a student has an unsuccessful project? Are you okay with them starting new projects or would you prefer they stick with their first idea?

Chapter 10

Keeping It Real

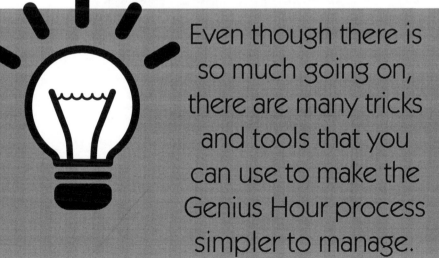

BIG IDEA

Even though there is so much going on, there are many tricks and tools that you can use to make the Genius Hour process simpler to manage.

As I've mentioned, Genius Hour is messy. It's stressful and not for the faint of heart. However, it is for those who want what is best for their students and are willing to take risks to encourage learning by application. The good news is, that even though there is so much going on, there are many tricks and tools that you can use to make the Genius Hour process simpler to manage and to track progress as your students work. This chapter details classroom management techniques, including strategies for post-Genius Hour cleanup, keeping students on track and monitoring progress, and ensuring projects remain student-driven. You will also find tips for assessing Genius Hour projects and getting support from administrators and parents.

Let It Go

Letting go of control is such an important part of making Genius Hour work. It will not be meaningful for our students if we continue to try to dictate and control what they are doing and how they do it. Let go of having to have all of the answers. Let go of that perfect lesson plan that never works out the way you intended anyway and let go of feeling like you are their only source of information. Because the reality is, you aren't.

My family and I recently went skiing in Angelfire, NM. It was the first time for our kids to ski and they had a blast. Our oldest, however, was too old for ski school so he only received half a day of training while the others received a full day. During our second day on the mountain, I was working with him and showing him how to stop. After trying several times and still not being as successful as he had hoped, he informed me that he wanted his little sister to teach him how to stop because he thought he could understand her better. Ouch! Really? I thought I was a great teacher and was doing a great job showing him how it was done. I had to let it go. And, believe it or not, after one or two times down the mountain with his sister, he had it down.

The same is true in our classrooms. Let them learn from each other. Don't feel like you have to know how to do something to allow them to try it. Learn with them and be willing to ask your students when you need help. The truth is, they may not need us make it down the mountain. Just having each other might be enough—and that's okay.

When Messes Are Made

With so many projects going on and so many materials being used, things can get messy very quickly. It's important to have procedures in place for organization. This looks different in every Genius Hour classroom. Some students store their materials in the classroom while others only bring their things on the days Genius Hour is happening. If students store their things in the classroom, it's best for every student to have an area. An area can be a cubby, box, or whatever works for you and your students. Students should know where their things are and be able to access them quickly.

Every student should take ownership and pride in keeping things running smoothly during Genius Hour time—and keeping things neat is a part of that.

Part of Genius Hour is the clean up at the end of the work period. In order to clean up appropriately, students need to know where things go and what they need to do. Although students working on digital projects might not have much to clean at the end of Genius Hour, students who are making a model volcano might have a lot to do. In order to support each other, encourage all students to help, even if it's not their project. For example, if all they needed to do was return their iPads to the cart, they can go help another group with clean up until it's all done.

Every student should take ownership and pride in keeping things running smoothly during Genius Hour time—and keeping things neat is a part of that. When something is spilled or a mess is made, students should be encouraged to help each other. Building a culture that appreciates the environment enough to take care of it is beneficial and gives students something to call their own. Teach them to respect their materials, the classroom, and each other by modeling and encouraging organization and respect for tools and materials used throughout the Genius Hour process.

Helping Students Stay on Track

The most important part of managing the Genius Hour process and the 6 P's is a bulletin board or other reference. Because the process is a cycle and students are working at their own pace, it is important for students to have something to refer back to when they feel lost. For our classroom, that was a 6 P's map on our bulletin board with information that was easy to access (see Figure 18).

I used colored cardstock and displayed the 6 P's along with a QR code for each. Creating QR codes is a very simple process and can be done very quickly. In order to do so, you can use a QR Code generator. There are many options to choose from and a quick

Figure 18. My classroom's Genius Hour bulletin board.

online search will give you access to a variety of choices, such as ForQRCode (https://forqrcode.com) or goQR.me (http://goqr.me). You can direct QR codes to a URL, PDF file, or other destination. Students can scan the codes with their smartphones or tablets, using a QR code scanner, such as QR Code Reader for iPhone or Android.

I attached each QR code that I created to a webpage on a class website. I created the website using Weebly (https://www.weebly. com), which is very easy to use. It is a drag-and-drop platform, making the process of building a website very simple. I created a page on the website for each of the 6 P's—passion, plan, pitch, project, product, and presentation. On each of the pages, I included information about that step in the process as well as a Google form for students to fill out. I used the forms as a way for me for me to keep up with where students were in the process and what they were working on at each step. For example, when they scanned the Product code, they were taken directly to a page with product examples, information, and a Google form asking what their final product was. I set the Google form up to notify me each time it was filled out so that I could keep up with who was doing what. If you use Google forms, this can be easily set up by going to the responses spreadsheet and setting up the notification rules.

Although a website is a great option, you could also develop a poster or PDF to guide students. (See Figure 1 for a sample student handout detailing the 6 P's.) If you use a PDF, you could even connect QR codes to the PDF with the information that students need for each of the steps in the Genius Hour process. When the QR code is scanned, students will have access to the document with the directions for what they need to do while on that step. Without QR codes, you could ensure that materials and information are in an accessible location in the classroom for students to easily find the resources that they need. Whatever strategy you choose will provide students with a place to find direction without always having to ask you what they need to be doing or where they can go to find information.

Monitoring Progress

As well as having students utilize Trello (https://trello.com) throughout the Genius Hour process, I also tracked student progress by using Trello myself. While the students used this tool to document their learning, I used it to keep track of which step students were on. I set up the lists—passion, plan, pitch, project, product,

Genius Hour Tracking					
Passion	**Plan**	**Pitch**	**Project**	**Product**	**Presentation**
Katy	Eli	Haley	James	Suzie	Alex
Cory	John	Joshua	Ally	Caitlyn	Carlos
Mary		Billy	Raquel		Amrita

Figure 19. Example student progress tracking board.

and presentation. Then, I added cards with student names. They all started out in the "passion" list, and I moved the cards as they moved through the process. Students can move the cards themselves if they have login information for Trello, or you can move the cards for them. Either way, this is an effective way to track where your students are and what they should be working on each day.

Figure 19 is an example of a student progress board. This could be done in the classroom by using index cards on a whiteboard or bulletin board. Students can physically move their cards as they move through the process. The names can even be erased and written under each of the 6 P's if an even simpler option is needed. There are many different ways to track where your students are in the process. In doing so, you will know where each student is and what they may need, making the process more manageable for yourself and meaningful for the students.

Genius Hour as Classwork, Not Homework

Many people ask if I ever assigned Genius Hour as homework. My students were not asked to work on their projects at home for several reasons. The first is that I wanted the project to be their work. Often times, homework becomes about just getting it done. I know this because I'm a mom and my kids have homework. Very rarely is homework meaningful and engaging. Getting work done at home is rushed and sometimes stressful for everyone involved. This is because we are a family of five and have a lot going on, just like every other family.

> In order for projects to be completely student-driven, I believe that they are best completed at school.

Genius Hour should not be stressful, and it should be done by the student. When a project is sent home, it is natural for parents to want to help. However, sometimes that help results in a need to "do it right" and will result in some of the student ownership being lost. In order for projects to be completely student-driven, I believe that they are best completed at school.

As many of us know, students, including gifted students, will sometimes become fixated on an idea, interest, or passion. If they are given the option to complete their projects at home, they will go home that night and complete the entire project before the next day. In order to work on the 4 C's + 1 R (see Chapter 2), students need to go through each of the 6 P's. The only way that you can monitor that process and see the work that is being done is to require that it is done in class.

Although I did not allow students to work on projects at home, I did allow them to perform certain tasks at home. For example, if a student needed to find some information by going to a local library or researching on his or her home computer, that was certainly allowed. I just wanted the product and most of the actual project portion of the process done in class. Believe me, most parents are just fine with this and will not request that you send anything home. Let's face it; most families have enough going on to keep them busy without throwing Genius Hour into the mix.

Assessing Projects

Grading Genius Hour projects can be tricky. Although it's important to make sure students are on task and making progress, I'm not sure that grades should be assigned to projects. I believe that feedback and conversation are the best ways to assess student learning throughout the Genius Hour process.

Instead of assessing the actual project, teachers can also assess development of important skills, like the 4 C's—collaboration, communication, creativity, and critical thinking. Through conversation and observation, teachers can see if students are improving their collaboration, communication, critical thinking, and creativity skills. There are many different 4 C rubric options online. My favorite rubrics for assessing the 4 C's in the elementary grades can be found at http://www.bhmschools.org/schools/tatanka/tatanka-stem-information/4cs-rubrics. Another great resource for finding rubrics appropriate for all grade levels, including presentation rubrics, is http://www.bie.org/objects/cat/rubrics. Find one that works for you and your students. Use the rubric as guide for assessment.

Feedback and conversation are the best ways to assess student learning throughout the Genius Hour process.

Self-assessment is an important skill that students need and can learn throughout this process as well. When using a 4 C rubric in my own classroom, I gave students an opportunity to share their thoughts before I completed the rubric to be shared with their parents. I filled out the rubric based on my observations and then asked the students to fill out the rubric themselves. When we were both done, we had a student-teacher conference and discussed our differences.

There were many instances in which the students gave themselves a lower score on the rubric than I had given them. This happened most often when we talked about collaboration. My gifted students explained to me that they were able to collaborate well in GT class with other gifted students. However, they felt like collaboration was a struggle in the regular classroom because they knew what was expected. They knew that they were expected to keep the group on track and make sure the right answers were given.

Don't assume that if you give students an opportunity to self-assess, they will give themselves high marks or better scores than they deserve. If a culture of trust is established, students will be willing to share their honest thoughts and become self-aware enough to be honest and forthcoming with their self-assessment.

Genius Hour is not about grades or assessment. The process is much more important than the product, and the feedback is more important than grades that are given along the way. If you are required to assess Genius Hour, however, consider any of the following as documentation:

- Trello boards or another strategy used to document student learning throughout the Genius Hour process (see Chapter 4, p. 42–43, and Chapter 6, p. 68);

- digital portfolios, such as FreshGrade (see Chapter 6, p. 77);

- rubrics completed by both the teacher and student to reflect progress;

- video reflections created by students to share learning; and/ or

- blog posts written by students during reflection time (see Chapter 6, p. 70).

Getting Buy-In From Parents

Allowing students to explore their passions is not something that parents will expect. It's important to prepare them for this type of learning and give them the advice that they need to encourage and support their children at home. Because you don't want parents to see Genius Hour as free time or fluff, they need to understand the why. They need to know that there is a process and know the reason behind Genius Hour being a priority in the classroom. Consider some of the following as you explain Genius Hour to your students' parents.

1. **Invite them in.** Don't be afraid to ask parents to visit your classroom. Make your classroom transparent and be willing to share anything and everything. Let them see what's working and what isn't. Share the good, the bad, and the ugly. Ask for suggestions and be willing to listen when they have ideas.

2. **Be honest.** Before starting Genius Hour, have a conversation. Invite parents to a meeting to discuss why you are going to make this priority, what you expect, and how they can help their students at home. Encourage them to simply

listen to their child talk about his or her project, and share questions that parents can ask to encourage reflection at home.

3. **Ask for help.** Parents are often more than willing to help when they know it is in the best interest of their child. Many parents will be very excited about the fact that their child is being given the opportunity to pursue his or her passion at school. Ask parents to send supplies, volunteer, or serve as outside experts for other students. Parent involvement builds classroom culture and means so much to the students. Encourage that involvement by being willing to ask for help and know your own limits.

Getting Buy-In From Administration

Many teachers have asked me how to "sell" Genius Hour to their administration. Unfortunately, not everyone sees the power of learning by doing. Many still believe that traditional learning is the best way for students to learn. I have had an opportunity to talk to many administrators and have had mixed reactions. However, I do believe that if Genius Hour is done correctly and the standards are the focus, it would be difficult for anyone to argue against the benefits that it has in the classroom.

That being said, I want to share a few suggestions when sharing Genius Hour with your administration and finding ways that it can be implemented in your own district, campus, or classroom.

1. **Be open minded.** Genius Hour is what you make it. There is not a right way for it to be done, and it doesn't have to be done the way that you've imagined for it to work. In other

words, if you would like to do Genius Hour every week but your administration only approves time for it once a month, that's okay. Take what you can get, and use that opportunity to invite administrators into your classroom to see how and why Genius Hour is so powerful.

2. **Understand their perspective.** Before approaching your administration about Genius Hour, put yourself in their position. As the principal or superintendent, what would your priorities be? Most administrators are open to new ideas, but they have seen many things come and go. They want to know what will work and why. How will Genius Hour help students make connections to the standards that have to be taught? If you can help them understand the power of making those connections and explain that the standards can still be a priority, most administrators will be willing to listen.

3. **Focus on big picture goals.** My friend, Scott Schweikhard, an administrator at Plano ISD, recently shared that the goal is to create lifelong learners, people who are going to learn long after they leave our classrooms and our schools. Helping others understand how Genius Hour creates an insatiable appetite that encourages students to seek knowledge and connections with experts helps them understand the why behind Genius Hour. As an administrator, he suggested that teachers talk to administration about big picture goals and help them understand that giving that time for Genius Hour will yield so much more down the road than simply giving more time for specific subject areas.

Final Thoughts

In closing, I would just like to share that you would be hard pressed to find a more meaningful experience to engage and encourage innovation in the classroom. Genius Hour can happen once a week, once during a 6-week period, or even once a semester. It's simply a matter of what works for you and your students. Genius Hour gives students an opportunity to learn through application. Application and reflection result in real learning, and in my opinion, that makes it worth every struggle, every chaotic minute, and every minute of my time. Seeing my students succeed or even fail while finding their passions has been the highlight of my educational career.

> Genius Hour can happen once a week, once during a 6-week period, or even once a semester. It's simply a matter of what works for you and your students.

Don't Feel Alone

Don't feel alone in the process. Become a connected educator by joining the conversation on Twitter (#geniushour) and sharing your experience with the community. Find educators to connect with and all of the information you will ever need as you begin the Genius Hour journey by referring to Joy Kirr's LiveBinder (http://www.livebinders.com/play/play?id=829279). The Genius Hour community is always growing, and new ideas are shared every day. It's no longer enough to simply provide lectures and worksheets about the information that we think students need. Our students need more than that. They deserve more than that. Creating opportunities for meaningful learning opportunities and giving our students the tools that they need to learn by doing has become a reality in so many classrooms. Education is changing, and I don't think any of us want to miss the chance to truly engage the learners who are in our classrooms every day.

Be Brave

Finally, be brave. Be brave enough to do what is best for your students instead of what is easy. Be brave enough to create a classroom that is designed for real learning by doing. See your students as the learners they are instead of the test scores you hope for them to be. Be brave enough to try something so different, so outside of the box, that it just might work for today's students. Be brave enough to learn with them and go on this journey together. Your students will never forget your willingness to do what was best for them, and you will never regret your decision to be the lead learner in your own classroom.

Reflection Questions

1. How will you manage the Genius Hour process? Will your system be digital or physical?

2. How do you feel about self-assessment? Do you believe that your students can self-assess effectively?

3. How do you feel about talking to your administration about Genius Hour?

4. If you are not connected to other educators through social media, what are some small steps you can take to make those connections?

5. What can you do in your classroom tomorrow for your students? What can you do to engage and ignite their passion for learning?

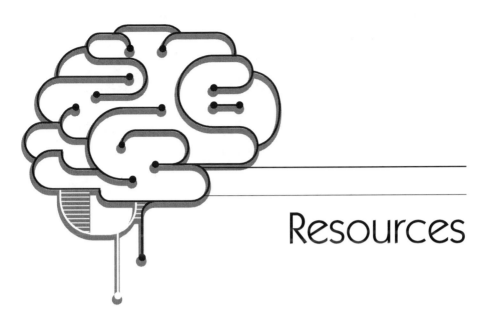

Resources

Print

***The Genius Hour Guidebook: Fostering Passion, Wonder, and Inquiry in the Classroom* by Denise Krebs and Gallit Zvi**

The Genius Hour Guidebook offers practical strategies and resources for implementing Genius Hour in the classroom. From developing inquiry questions to presenting finished products, it is full of ideas to help you plan and carry out Genius Hour with your students.

***Inquiry and Innovation in the Classroom: Using 20% Time, Genius Hour, and PBL to Drive Student Success* by A. J. Juliani**

In Juliani's book, he shares how Genius Hour can help foster innovation and inquiry in the classroom, preparing students for the real world. He shares real examples and real stories, making it easy for teachers to understand how Genius Hour can be a reality in their classrooms.

***The Passion-Driven Classroom: A Framework for Teaching and
Learning* by Angela Maiers and Amy Sandvold**

The Passion-Driven Classroom helps teachers understand the importance of igniting a love for learning in their students by sharing specific ideas and activities to allow passion to drive learning.

***Pure Genius: Building a Culture of Innovation and Taking 20%
Time to the Next Level* by Don Wettrick**

Pure Genius explains how innovation has the power to change education. Don's book inspires educators to focus on student passions and help them find opportunity. Reading this book will help you realize the importance of social media, innovation in schools, and collaboration both in and out of the classroom.

Online

Websites

Engage Their Minds (Genius Hour Resources)
https://engagetheirminds.com/genius-hour-resources

Terri Eichholz has created some wonderful resources to be used with Genius Hour. Some of those resources include a Genius Hour trailer, log, and planner.

Genius Hour
http://www.geniushour.com

This website is a great place to learn more about the basics of Genius Hour. I love to use this website and the video included to introduce Genius Hour to parents and staff wanting to know more about the process.

Genius Hour/20% Time by Joy Kirr
http://www.livebinders.com/play/play?id=829279

Kirr's Livebinder is Genius Hour heaven! Everything you would ever need to implement Genius Hour in your classroom can be found here. She works hard to curate Genius Hour resources that are shared on social media and blogs. This is by far one of the best Genius Hour resources that exists today.

"Reflection Facilitated by QR Codes" by Tony Vincent
http://learninginhand.com/blog/2013/7/5/roll-reflect-with-qr-codes

These reflection codes, created by Tony Vincent, are a lifesaver when teaching students to reflect effectively. The randomly generated reflection questions require students to truly reflect instead of simply remembering what they are working on.

"Step-by-Step Directions for Creating Passion Projects in Our Classroom" by Paul Solarz
http://psolarz.weebly.com/mr-solarz-eportfolio/step-by-step-directions-for-creating-passion-projects-in-our-classroom

Paul Solarz does a great job showcasing student work and sharing what he is doing in his own classroom. His website includes actual student work and examples, making it easy for teachers to see what can be expected as they implement Genius Hour.

"Upgrade Your KWL Chart to the 21st Century" by Langwitches
http://langwitches.org/blog/2011/07/21/upgrade-your-kwl-chart-to-the-21st-century

This post shares how to take KWL charts to the next level. In doing so, students are given the opportunity to reflect on their project as well as focus on what they will be learning when getting started.

Social Media

Join the #geniushour chat on Twitter (first Thursday of each month at https://twitter.com/hashtag/GeniusHour), and follow Genius Hour leaders:

Terri Eichholz (@terrieichholz)
https://twitter.com/terrieichholz

Terri Eichholz is an educator whose experience and knowledge is based on implementing all that she posts about in her own classroom. Terri also has a wonderful blog (https://engagetheirminds.com) and shares some wonderful tools to use with Genius Hour. Her tools are easy to use and can be implemented immediately.

A. J. Juliani (@ajjuliani)
https://twitter.com/ajjuliani

A. J. Juliani is an educator who not only writes and shares about Genius Hour but implements it in his own classroom. He has written several books and often shares the power of innovation in the classroom.

Joy Kirr (@joykirr)
https://twitter.com/joykirr

Joy Kirr can often be found on the #geniushour hashtag retweeting and sharing ideas. She does amazing things for the Genius Hour community and works hard to make sure we have access to what other teachers and Genius Hour advocates are doing.

Denise Krebs (@mrsdkrebs)
https://twitter.com/mrsdkrebs

Gallit Zvi (@gallit_z)
https://twitter.com/gallit_z

Gallit and Denise moderate the #geniushour Twitter chat on the first Thursday of each month. They are the Genius Hour gurus who have led the way for so many of us to make Genius Hour a reality in our classrooms.

Hugh McDonald (@hughtheteacher)
https://twitter.com/hughtheteacher

Hugh has a wonderful blog (https://hughtheteacher.wordpress.com) and is another educator who led the way when so many of us were just learning about Genius Hour and finding ways to use it in our classrooms.

Don Wettrick (@donwettrick)
https://twitter.com/donwettrick

Don is an amazing educator in Indiana who teaches an Innovations class. Following him will inspire you to get of your comfort zone and do what is best for students. He is a thought-leader in education and changing what today's classroom looks like.

Videos

***"2013 Genius Hour Reflections"* by Joy Kirr**
https://www.youtube.com/watch?v=TTRZ5YgghfM

This video, featuring Joy Kirr's students reflecting on Genius Hour, is a great tool to share with other teachers—or even students—when introducing them to Genius Hour and its benefits.

"*Genius Hour*" by Big Brain Academy
https://www.youtube.com/watch?v=FEQzKH7v0-Q

This animated video, by Big Brain Academy, is a quick and easy-to-follow introductory guide to Genius Hour to share with students in the classroom.

"*What Is Genius Hour?—Introduction to Genius Hour in the Classroom*" by Chris Kesler
https://www.youtube.com/watch?v=NMFQUtHsWhc

This video is a guide for teachers who want to learn the basics of Genius Hour.

The Technology to Make It Happen

Blogger
https://www.blogger.com

Blogger is a free blogging platform that is very easy to use. Teachers and students alike can utilize the platform to share posts with the public. Teachers can share their experiences and ideas with other educators on a classroom blog, or students can use the platform to share and reflect on their progress throughout their Genius Hour project.

Book Creator
http://bookcreator.com

This app is a wonderful tool for creating digital books. Book Creator offers an alternative to writing a book using paper and pencil or older platforms and gives students many opportunities to be creative.

DIY

https://diy.org

DIY is an amazing place for students to explore their interests. By exploring the patches, they are given challenges to learn more about skills that might be interesting to them. This is a great place to start when introducing Genius Hour.

DOGO News: Fodder for Young Minds

http://www.dogonews.com

DOGO News offers current events that are written specifically for students. Articles are appropriate, interesting, and include lots of images and videos.

DonorsChoose.org

https://www.donorschoose.org

DonorsChoose.org is a wonderful organization that gives teachers an opportunity to write requests for funding for materials they need in the classroom. Most projects receive full funding.

Facebook

https://www.facebook.com

Facebook is the social network that allows users to like, comment, and share posts. Teachers can use the platform to connect with other educators, whereas students can use it to reach authentic audiences.

FreshGrade

https://www.freshgrade.com

FreshGrade is a platform for digital portfolios that offers students an opportunity to share their progress as well as reflect on what they have accomplished. Teachers and parents are able to comment and offer feedback using this tool, which results in meaningful learning for the student.

Google Hangouts

https://hangouts.google.com

Hangouts allow users to video chat using a webcam. The number of people in a Hangout is limited to 10, but a Hangout is a great way to communicate with outside experts who cannot physically visit with students.

Google Slides

https://www.google.com/slides/about

Google Slides is a very simple alternative to Microsoft Power Point. Google Slides can be shared and students can collaborate even when working on different computers.

iMovie

http://www.apple.com/imovie

iMovie is an app that allows students to create trailers or movies. The trailers are already created and students can choose the theme and simply drop in their own media. iMovie is a great way to create a nice presentation in a short amount of time.

Instagram

https://www.instagram.com

Instagram is a social media platform on which students and teachers can share images with authentic audiences.

KidBlog

http://kidblog.org

KidBlog is a wonderful blogging platform for students. Because teachers can moderate the comments, this is a safe tool that students find very easy to use.

littleBits

http://littlebits.cc

littleBits are electronic building blocks that help students understand circuits and engineering. littleBits encourage students to innovate, create, and build using science, technology, engineering, and math skills.

Mindmeister

https://www.mindmeister.com

Mindmeister is a mind-mapping tool for students to use when planning or brainstorming.

Nepris

https://nepris.com

Nepris connects industry experts with the classroom. By completing a form, educators are given access to experts that they can virtually invite into the classroom, providing real-world connections and addressing specific standards.

Padlet
https://padlet.com

Padlet is a very similar to a digital bulletin board. Students post on the board and their responses show up in real time.

Popplet
http://popplet.com

Popplet is a very simple mind-mapping tool. It gives students a blank canvas to create a diagram that represents their ideas throughout the planning stage of Genius Hour.

PowToon
https://www.powtoon.com

Powtoon allows students to create animated slideshows. Students love to create using PowToon because there are so many options and such a variety of animations that they can use.

Prezi
https://prezi.com

Prezi is an alternative to PowerPoint that brings presentations to life. The visual aspect of Prezi makes it fun for students to use, as they are able to be creative and design a presentation that engages the audience.

Qr Code Generator
http://www.qr-code-generator.com

This is a great tool that can be used to create QR codes. QR codes are quick response codes that can be scanned in order to visit a website, obtain information, or even share an image or video. This is my favorite QR code creator just because it is very easy to find and use.

Reflection Facilitated by QR Codes

http://learninginhand.com/blog/2013/7/5/roll-reflect-with-qr-codes

These QR codes provide random reflection questions for students as they begin to learn what reflection is and how it is different from remembering. Giving students access to these QR codes will encourage them to think differently about their work and make connections between what they have done and what they have learned.

Scratch

https://scratch.mit.edu

Scratch is a tool that was created by MIT to help students learn how to code. The tools uses blocks that students connect to create an algorithm. In doing so, they begin to learn how to write code on a very basic level. Students can create video games, animations, and more using Scratch.

Skype

https://www.skype.com

Skype is a tool that can be used to video chat with outside experts. It is popular and used by many businesses to connect with others outside of their organization. All that is needed is a Skype account and a webcam.

Trello

https://trello.com

Trello is an organization tool that students and teachers can use to organize information, resources, and more. It is simply a board with lists that are created by the user. This is a great way to store information and track learning as students work on their Genius Hour projects.

Twitter

https://twitter.com

Twitter is a social media platform that allows users to post short tweets that can be 140 characters in length. Twitter is a great place to connect and collaborate with educators all over the world. Students can also use the platform to connect with outside experts and authentic audiences.

Vidra

http://tentouchapps.com/vidra

Vidra is an easy-to-use app in which students can quickly develop presentations.

Weebly

https://www.weebly.com

Weebly is a great tool for creating websites. It is a drag and drop tool making it easy for both students and teachers to use. Weebly is very user-friendly and gives students an opportunity to be creative and make changes as they create and design a website.

Weebly for Education

https://education.weebly.com

Weebly for Education is just as wonderful as Weebly. It is easy to set up and gives your students a place to store their websites. You will have access to their work, and they will be able to log in through a student portal.

Wonderopolis

http://wonderopolis.org

Wonderopolis is an amazing website that shares a new wonder every day. These wonders include images, video, and a short article about that day's wonder. Each article also includes a vocabulary challenge and short quiz to check for understanding. Students can also access the archive for information about specific topics.

WordPress

https://wordpress.com

Wordpress is a great blog- and/or website-building tool for students or teachers. I recommend it for secondary students because of its real-world applications. Many businesses use Wordpress to run their websites.

YouTube

https://www.youtube.com

YouTube allows users to share videos. Channels are created, and work is uploaded and can be shared publicly, with specific individuals, or kept private.

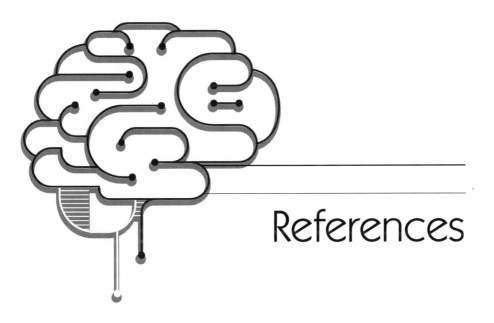

References

Adams, S. (2014). The 10 skills employers most want in 2015 graduates. *Forbes*. Retrieved from http://www.forbes.com/sites/susanadams/2014/11/12/the-10-skills-employers-most-want-in-2015-graduates

Feitlinger, S. B. (2016, February 26). The battery of the future may be made of paper! *DOGO News*. Retrieved from http://www.dogonews.com/2016/2/26/the-battery-of-the-future-may-be-made-of-paper

Juliani, A. J. (2013). *6 simple strategies to help find your passion.* Retrieved from http://ajjuliani.com/6-simple-strategies-to-help-find-your-passion

Minock, D. (2013). *Two guys and some iPads: The two guys show #12* [Video file]. Retrieved from http://www.twoguysandsomeipads.com/2013/11/the-two-guys-show-12-donwettrick.html

National Education Association. (2010). *Preparing 21st century students for a global society: An educator's guide to the "four Cs".* Retrieved from http://www.nea.org/assets/docs/A-Guide-to-Four-Cs.pdf

Pappas, P. (2010). A taxonomy of reflection: Critical thinking for students, teachers, and principals (part 1). *Copy/Paste.* Retrieved from http://www.peterpappas.com/2010/01/taxonomy-reflection-critical-thinking-students-teachers-principals.html

Solarz, P. (2013). Step-by-step directions for creating passion projects in our classroom. *What's Going on in Mr. Solarz' Class?* Retrieved from http://psolarz.weebly.com/mr-solarz-eportfolio/step-by-step-directions-for-creating-passion-projects-in-our-classroom

Tolisano, S. (2011). Upgrade your KWL chart to the 21st century. *Langwitches.* Retrieved from http://langwitches.org/blog/2011/07/21/upgrade-your-kwl-chart-to-the-21st-century

Vincent, T. (2013). Reflection facilitated by QR codes. *Learning in Hand.* Retrieved from http://learninginhand.com/blog/2013/7/5/roll-reflect-with-qr-codes

About the Author

Andi McNair was a classroom teacher for 13 years before finding her passion as a gifted education specialist. She spent many years teaching at the small school from which she graduated and loved being part of a small community that supported innovation in the classroom.

Andi is married to her junior high sweetheart. They live in a Valley Mills, TX, where they are raising their three children. She is a mother of gifted children and understands the need for advocacy and support for gifted education.

Recently, Andi became the Digital Innovation Specialist at ESC Region 12. Last year, she was named one of the Top People in Education to Watch in 2016 by the Academy of Education Arts and Sciences. Andi absolutely loves sharing her passion for innovative education with other teachers who want more for their students. Visit her website at http://www.andimcnair.com.